DIXIEBALL

One hears much in these days of the New South. The land of the storied rebel becomes industrialized; it casts up a new aristocracy of money-bags which in turn spawns a new *noblesse;* scoriac ferments spout and thunder toward an upheaval and overturn of all the old social, political, and intellectual values and an outgushing of divine fire in the arts—these are the things one hears about. There is a new South, to be sure. It is a chicken-pox of factories on the Watch-Us-Grow maps; it is a kaleidoscopic chromo of stacks and chimneys on the club-car window as the train rolls southward from Washington to New Orleans.

But I question that it is much more. For the mind of that heroic region, I opine, is still basically and essentially the mind of the Old South. It is a mind, that is to say, of the soil rather than of the mills—a mind, indeed, which, as yet, is almost wholly unadjusted to the new industry.

—**W. J. CASH,** *The Mind of the South*

DIXIE**BALL**

Race and Professional Basketball
in the Deep South, 1947–1979

THOMAS AIELLO

SPORT AND POPULAR CULTURE   Brian M. Ingrassia, Series Editor

University of Tennessee Press / Knoxville

Library of Congress Cataloging-in-Publication Data

Names: Aiello, Thomas, 1977– author.
Title: Dixieball: race and professional basketball in the Deep South,
    1947–1979 / Thomas Aiello.
Description: First edition. | Knoxville: University of Tennessee Press,
    [2018] | Series: Sport and popular culture | Includes bibliographical
    references and index. |
Identifiers: LCCN 2018029990 (print) | LCCN 2018039733 (ebook) |
    ISBN 9781621904649 (Kindle) | ISBN 9781621904656 (pdf) |
    ISBN 9781621904632 (hardcover)
Subjects: LCSH: Basketball—Southern States—History. | Racism in
    sports—Southern States—History.
Classification: LCC GV885.72.S85 (ebook) | LCC GV885.72.S85 A54 2018
    (print) | DDC 796.323/640975—dc23
LC record available at https://lccn.loc.gov/2018029990

CONTENTS

FOREWORD

In 1959, as the centennial of the Civil War approached, there were no major-league sports teams in the South. No Major League Baseball (MLB), National Football League (NFL), National Basketball Association (NBA), or National Hockey League (NHL) franchises existed in the eleven states that had seceded to form the Confederacy nearly a century earlier. Zero. Of course, there were significant minor-league baseball teams like the Atlanta Crackers and Birmingham Barons—the latter of which once had its games called by one Theophilus Eugene "Bull" Connor. And there were big-time intercollegiate teams at the Universities of Alabama, North Carolina, Tennessee, Virginia, and other SEC or ACC schools, none of which had yet begun to integrate. But the major leagues—which then had, as Thomas Aiello notes, a combined forty-two teams—were absent. Not until 1960 would a former Confederate state see its first major-league franchise: the Dallas Cowboys. The movement of major-league teams into southern states only got more complicated in a postwar era when Jackie Robinson and other pioneering black athletes worked to break down sporting "color lines" established since the 1800s.

Things started to change in the 1960s, the decade when Dr. Martin Luther King, Jr., jailed for the supposed crime of parading without a permit, wrote in his famous "Letter from Birmingham Jail" how African Americans living in Jim Crow America were not able to enjoy the relatively prosperous postwar decades the same as white Americans. Black children could not have fun at the same amusement parks as white children; black travelers could not find equal accommodations along the new Interstate Highways. Something seemed amiss when people in postcolonial African nations sped toward liberty but their American brothers and sisters begged for the right to purchase a cup of coffee. The United States would not really fulfill the promise of the Emancipation Proclamation—or the dream King proclaimed at the 1963 March on Washington—until black and white Americans could work and play equally.

Thomas Aiello shows us in his masterful *Dixieball* that the South made progress in sports desegregation in the era of civil rights and Black Power, but this progress was neither as smooth nor quick as it could have been. White supremacy died hard in sport—the same as in just about every other aspect of southern (really, American) life. *Dixieball* examines the early story of professional basketball in Atlanta and New Orleans—historically, two of the South's major transportation hubs and cultural centers—to show us just how much white southerners wanted professional sports franchises; at the same time, they were not willing to surrender racial superstitions. The Deep South, it turns out, had a difficult time embracing a sport with a long history of black athleticism and sweaty, body-to-body contact in inner-city gymnasiums.

Since the days of Mayor William B. Hartsfield, Atlanta has liked to bill itself as the "City Too Busy to Hate." This was never quite true, especially in the 1960s, but it was a narrative that helped the Gate City open the door to professional sports. While Birmingham became notorious as the city of Bull Connor's snarling police dogs and skin-peeling firehoses, Atlanta's reputation for less openly hateful race relations, along with tremendous postwar growth, helped attract major-league sports franchises like the MLB Braves and NFL Falcons (both 1966), as well as the NBA Hawks, who moved to Atlanta from St. Louis in turbulent 1968. New Orleans, the fabled port city at the Mississippi's mouth, has a long history as a place where racial divisions may have been more loosely drawn than elsewhere in the Deep South. The Crescent City experimented with professional sports with the New Orleans Buccaneers of the upstart American Basketball Association (ABA) in 1967, the same year the NFL's Saints came marching in, but it landed on the NBA map with the arrival of the expansion-franchise Jazz in 1974. By expertly crafting the story of professional basketball coming to these two cities during the 1960s and 1970s, Aiello complicates simple narratives about race, desegregation, and civil rights. Neither city, as it turns out, was quite ready to abandon the sports-contracts of whiteness.

At the center of this enthralling story is Pete "the Pistol" Maravich, a basketball prodigy who became legendary while playing for his father at Louisiana State University in the late 1960s. Soon, white fans across Dixie embraced Maravich as basketball's "Great White Hope," the hoopster who might return white America to hardwood glory. This was a time when the NBA was still an up-and-coming league, fighting off the ABA's challenge. There were athletic-shoe endorsements, but nothing like what Americans would see in the era of Michael Jordan and Nike. Rather, it was a time when some Americans thought professional basketball was too "black" to be truly popular. This was a time of Bill Russell, Wilt Chamberlain, and Kareem Abdul-Jabbar. Maravich seemed to be the player who would prove that white men could jump—and run and dribble and score, too. *Dixieball* follows Maravich from Baton Rouge to Atlanta and the Big Easy, but it focuses more on Maravich's meanings than his maverick style of play. The Pistol's lavish paychecks proved that whiteness could be immensely profitable for a basketball prodigy of the right ancestry. But they also proved to be poor business for cities hoping to profit from professional sports. Like Ahab chasing the white whale, New Orleans's 1970s pro-basketball dreams were shattered when the Jazz mortgaged their future on Maravich. Meanwhile, Atlanta adopted a more Ishmael-like racial openness by the 1980s and its NBA team thrived.

Thomas Aiello is a talented scholar and writer who has published on a wide array of social and cultural history topics, ranging from the Grambling-Southern football rivalry to baseball in the Great Depression. He has a keen eye for detail and a voice that conveys the motivations and compulsions of historical actors without asking us to let them off the hook for the consequences of their actions. *Dixieball* pulls us back into an era that is puzzlingly familiar yet sometimes shockingly different from our own. We see the casual racism of Morton Downey Jr.—perhaps the individual most instrumental in bringing New Orleans its first pro basketball team in the 1960s—alongside his desire for racial equality. We are also reminded of the racist imagery of restaurant chain Sambo's, which floundered at the same time its owners saw the fortunes of their NBA franchise sink into oblivion.

Dixieball also provides valuable insights regarding arena construction in relation to economic development and race relations in post-1960s American cities. Sunbelt metropolises like Atlanta and New Orleans hoped to pull themselves into the major leagues, but they needed places to play. Initially, ABA and NBA franchises arranged with colleges or municipal auditoriums for their games. But the politics of arena construction ultimately led to battles over the siting and managing of venues such as the Superdome in New Orleans.

Today, thirty-two major-league sports teams play in states of the former Confederacy: five in MLB, nine in the NFL, nine in the NBA, five in the NHL, and four in Major League Soccer (MLS), a league whose existence was nearly unthinkable in the 1960s. Of course, America's race problems have not disappeared, and we fool ourselves if we think otherwise. National-anthem protests in the NFL like those led by Colin Kaepernick have prompted ugly white-supremacist backlash. Meanwhile, the racial politics of American cities continue to influence placement of new sports venues. But as civil-rights icon and Georgia Congressman John Lewis once said about his experiences in a post-Freedom Ride era, "things have changed." Let's tip the ball to Thomas Aiello so we can learn more about the early stages of that transformation in Deep South sports.

Brian M. Ingrassia
West Texas A&M University

INTRODUCTION

Organized professional basketball began in the mid-1920s, far from the Jim Crow gymnasiums of the Deep South, when the American Basketball League attempted to formalize various professional contests and barnstorming events throughout the North into something more manageable. In 1946, the Basketball Association of America (BAA) replaced the American Basketball League. Meanwhile, the National Basketball League (NBL) was founded in 1937, creating a talent and attendance war between the two groups. In 1948, the BAA finally got the upper hand in the feud by stealing away four of the NBL's teams, including Rochester, the league's champion, and Minneapolis, which featured the league's best player, George Mikan. The secessions weakened the NBL, which agreed to a merger the following season. In 1949 the National Basketball Association (NBA) was formed, and it received its own competitive rival in the 1960s, the American Basketball Association (ABA). The ABA forced yet another merger in the following decade.[1]

When the University of San Francisco's Bill Russell arrived in the NBA in the 1950s, professional teams were reluctant to sign black players. Though they were far from the South, the teams feared alienating their predominantly white customer base. Meanwhile, the Harlem Globetrotters, at the height of their popularity and competitive powers, were often able to outbid league teams for black players. Russell changed that dynamic, if slowly. He was a collegiate and Olympic champion with name recognition. He also made the Boston Celtics a perennial power and provided the NBA with newfound popularity and economic stability. As Boston sportswriter Bob Ryan explains, signing Russell over the siren song of the Globetrotters "did not prove to be difficult." Ryan credits Russell's competitive makeup with creating his desire "to play in the world's strongest basketball league rather than become a full-time clown." While such conclusions are unfair to the Globetrotters, Russell's decision served as the axis point upon which the success of the NBA and the marginalization of barnstorming teams turned. Moreover, his choice served as the entry point into the association for black players of lesser talent and lesser name recognition.[2]

And then there was the Deep South. Far from Harlem, Rochester, Minneapolis, and Boston, the southern Closed Society, in the words of James W. Silver, discussing Mississippi in 1964, "has been on the defensive against inexorable change for more than a century." It was a society whose "all-pervading doctrine, then and now, has been white supremacy, whether achieved through slavery or segregation," a society "requiring that nonconformists and dissenters from the code be silenced, or, in a crisis, driven from the community."[3]

It was not that intransigence that made the South an unwelcome market for major-league professional sports prior to World War II. Those sports served as their own versions of closed societies that toed a distinct racial line. Rather, the South was a region of small markets far from the hubs of professional sports in the Northeast and Midwest. After the war, however, race policy became a legitimate bar to professional sports for growing southern metropolitan areas. For example, as the Basketball Association of America was forming in 1946, Jackie Robinson arrived in Sanford, Florida, for his first spring training with the Brooklyn Dodgers. But the racial animus about an integrated team in the town was so virulent, so ugly, that the Dodgers sought a safer, more hospitable climate in Daytona Beach.[4] The Closed Society brooked no such crossings of the racial line, even if such a stance meant the loss of a financial windfall. The long history of the postbellum South, from the failure of Populist politics to spending on segregated facilities to out-of-state tuition vouchers for black graduate students, demonstrated a quick willingness to sacrifice its own economic best interests to maintain white supremacy.

But there were holes in that wall of intransigence. In 1947, the year after Robinson was run out of Sanford, Toledo basketball promoter Sid Goldberg scheduled a professional barnstorming tour of the South. New Orleans and Atlanta fielded teams in the upstart Professional Basketball League of America. And other cities in the South developed an opportunity for professional basketball through the creation of the Southern Basketball League. Still, despite the efforts, the barnstorming tour was a failure, and both leagues collapsed. And none of those teams were integrated. None had the imprimatur of racial progress as did, say, the Dodgers.

In 1950, only forty-two major-league professional franchises existed, and these were located mostly in a tier of industrial states that extended from the Northeast to the Midwest. Sunbelt cities Los Angeles and San Francisco got professional football teams in 1946. For baseball, relocation came before expansion, as owners in cities with two teams began to spread out. In 1953, the Boston Braves moved to Milwaukee, and in 1954, the St. Louis Browns moved to Baltimore. The following year, the Philadelphia Athletics moved to Kansas City. In 1958, two years after the retirement of Jackie Robinson, the Brooklyn Dodgers and the New York Giants moved to Los Angeles and San Francisco, respectively.

In professional basketball, the Buffalo Bisons moved to Moline, Illinois, in 1946, becoming the Tri-Cities Blackhawks. The team moved to Milwaukee and became the Hawks in 1951, then moved to St. Louis in 1955. In 1945, the Rochester Royals developed out of an upstate New York semi-professional team, winning the NBA championship in 1951 before moving to Cincinnati in 1957. Leagues moving to Sunbelt cities and to the edge of the South in the postwar years responded to new urban growth, the advent of easy and relatively affordable jet airplane travel, the development of the interstate highway system, and other methods of cheap, reliable transportation.[5]

What ultimately began to open the Closed Society to professional sports, however, was less the possibility of progress that came with such teams and more that the racial barricades that blocked them were crumbling. The civil rights movement of the 1950s and 1960s broadcast the Deep South's white supremacy into every home in the country, ultimately generating federal initiatives to wrest racial decisions out of the hands of locals. In 1964, the Civil Rights Act became the exclamation point on a civil rights sentence that had begun a decade prior on a Montgomery bus. But this legislation did not automatically open the doors of the Deep South. In June of the following year, for example, the year the federal Voting Rights Act became law, Atlanta sought and received an NFL franchise, knowing that the team would be integrated. Two months prior, however, an all-white jury had acquitted Lester Maddox for taking an ax handle to black protesters at his all-white Pickwick Restaurant in Atlanta. This kind of action would launch his white supremacist reactionary political career in the years to come. Furthermore, New Orleans sought and received the American Football League's All-Star Game in 1965, but the racial animus of the city's residents toward black athletes ultimately led to a boycott. The event was canceled and moved to nearby Houston.

The controversies demonstrated a Deep South in the throes of change, a region in which cities tried to remove themselves from the Closed Society and become part of the business-minded Sunbelt. Cities hoped to take advantage of those loosed fetters of segregation laws to encourage a new economic success and erase the tainted reputation earned over the previous decade of civil rights struggles. But the racial animus generating those struggles still lingered, making that transition difficult.

One of the hallmarks of that new economic success was the South's acquisition of professional sports teams. In 1966, the year after the Maddox acquittal and the birth of the Atlanta Falcons, the Milwaukee Braves began play in Atlanta. The month after the baseball season ended, in November 1966, New Orleans received its own NFL franchise, which would begin play the following season. Professional basketball, however, was functionally different from baseball and football. Fans were closer to the players, who showed more of their bodies and had nothing covering their face and head. Blackness, then, had more of an impact in basketball than it had in other sports, and professional basketball was blackening. When Rosa Parks was removed from her Montgomery bus, the NBA was 7.5 percent black. By the time Lyndon Johnson signed the Voting Rights Act, it was 47.5 percent black. Professional basketball, despite integrating after baseball and football, was becoming known as a "black" sport.

That being the case, the Sunbelt South's relationship with professional basketball was more fraught, more representative of its slow crawl from the social and economic prison of the Closed Society, as the business imperatives and cultural currency that came with professional sports clashed with the undeniable blackness of basketball. It was a conflict that made the survival of those teams more tenuous, the fan support more fickle, and the racial incidents between players and fans more hostile. Professional basketball's first move to the Deep South was problematic and largely temporary. Racism clashed with civic development in a new and changing region.

Such conclusions ultimately challenge the assertions of economist David George Surdam and his otherwise vital and comprehensive 2012 business history of the NBA. While Surdam notes the difficulties black players suffered in the NBA, he argues for a "generally benign picture of integration" in the association. He acknowledges black athletes' questions about quotas and race-based restrictions on play, but argues that "there was no 'white flight' of fans from the NBA's changing complexion. All things considered, the NBA did a credible job of integrating." He ultimately concludes that "fans did not avoid games with African American players," that "white players appeared to have largely accepted black players as both teammates and opponents," and that "whatever discrimination occurred seemed to be aimed at the black players who were not among the elite."[6] *Dixieball*'s depiction of the clash between civic development and racism in the Deep South directly contradicts such assertions.

To demonstrate the evolution of that clashing, *Dixieball* begins by describing the intersections of professional basketball and the Deep South in the two decades prior to the region's first major franchise. Chapter 1 starts with Goldberg's barnstorming tour and the early postwar leagues that included southern teams, and continues through a series of racial incidents during NBA tours through the South that radicalized Bill Russell, Elgin Baylor, and others. Such episodes portended failure for future professional relationships with the region. Chapter 2 describes the birth of the first major Deep South professional basketball team, the New Orleans Buccaneers of the American Basketball Association, from its creation by, of all people, Morton Downey Jr. to its move away from the city three years later.

Chapter 3 examines the St. Louis Hawks' successful move to Atlanta, where a consistently winning team was dismantled. White southern talent replaced black stars so that the Hawks would be more marketable to a white fanbase who wanted to see white players. The effort culminated in the acquisition of the Great White Hope, LSU's Pete Maravich. Chapter 4 evaluates the next NBA team to arrive in the Deep South, the expansion New Orleans Jazz. The newly created team immediately leveraged its future to acquire the home-state boy, Atlanta's Great White Hope, to serve a similar role for its own franchise. The results were just as disastrous. Without the legacy of an established tradition, the Jazz absconded from the Deep South in 1979. Its owners, an absentee group from California headed by a devout Mormon, moved the team to smaller but more affluent Salt Lake City.

That year, the racial dynamic in the Deep South's relationship with professional basketball would begin to change. As the Jazz moved west, a new freshman player, Dominique Wilkins, began his collegiate career at the University of Georgia. While the Jazz would draft Wilkins first, he would soon after join the Atlanta Hawks and become the Deep South's first transcendent black basketball star. Fans in Atlanta would always see Wilkins as a Bulldog and an SEC alumnus first, thereby easing his transition to superstardom in the South. A legitimate devotion for the Wilkins-led Hawks resulted. It made professional basketball cool and ultimately paved the way in the early twenty-first century, three years after Wilkins's retirement, for a new, more stable franchise in New Orleans. An interrelated series of social and cultural forces that made the 1980s South a fundamentally different place than the 1960s South also facilitated Wilkins's arrival in professional basketball. White Georgians who welcomed him had experienced more than a decade of integrated high school and collegiate basketball. They had cheered Hank Aaron as he broke baseball's home run record in 1974 and Herschel Walker as he led the University of Georgia to a 1980 national championship

and a 1982 Heisman Trophy. While acceptance of black citizens' equal participation in society had not yet fully penetrated the white South, an acceptance
of exceptional black athletes' stardom had.

The South's move from a Closed Society to a region that embraced professional basketball was slow and complex, its story often ignored because of
the status of baseball or the popularity of football. But basketball was the
one professional sport that came south with an established and overt racial
identity. Its inculcation was the most difficult of the three sports. But it
was also the most telling as to the evolution of racial attitudes among white
sports fans in the Deep South, demonstrating that eighty years after the
demise of the Populists and the triumph of *Plessy v. Ferguson*, reputation
could finally trump race in southern civic engagement. And everyone could
go watch a game.

1

THROUGH THE RACIAL LOOKING GLASS

"I liked Sid Goldberg," said Tom Falvey, former president of Toledo Golden Gloves. "He was one of the best promoters around these parts." Goldberg promoted more than a hundred boxing cards in Toledo, Ohio, and he also worked as a circulation manager for the local paper. But his first love was basketball. In 1947, Goldberg staged a series of professional games in the South. He had been an owner, a coach, and a general manager for several professional teams in Toledo, and that year, he was leading the Toledo Jeeps in the National Basketball League. The Jeeps were unsuccessful, as Goldberg's Toledo White Huts had been earlier in the decade. Like his stint as general manager in Ohio basketball, Goldberg's promotional tour through the South was a near-total failure. Crowds in New Orleans and Houston seemed excited about the opportunity. But no one else did. Atlanta was perhaps the most inhospitable city, drawing only eighty-four paying customers. "We thought Atlanta was a Ku Klux Klan city," Goldberg remembered. "And our teams had mostly Jewish players."[1]

Disinterest and discrimination were the twin marks against the southern expansion of major-league professional sports, but Goldberg's southern counterparts still wanted professional teams in the region. In acquiring professional sports franchises, the postwar Sunbelt South generated revenue and spurred urban building renewal. The region also validated the civic growth that had already taken place. In 1947, for example, New Orleans and Atlanta were still hypersegregated cities, but they had a chance at major-league professional sports with the creation of the Professional Basketball League of America. The league was the brainchild of Maurice A. White, a Chicago businessman and promoter whose Chicago American Gears basketball team had won the older National League title the previous season.[2]

After their victory, White pulled the Gears from the National to start his own organization. He named lawyer and banker Holland Pile, also from Chicago, as commissioner, and Pile's offices in Chicago regulated salaries, schedules, and transportation for all of the included teams. Even Goldberg had a brief stint as a league executive that fall. The Professional Basketball League of America's northern division featured various teams in the Midwest. Its southern division—despite Goldberg's failed exhibition tour earlier that year—placed franchises in Atlanta, Birmingham, Chattanooga, and New Orleans, along with a western contingent of teams in Houston, Oklahoma City, Tulsa, and Springfield, Missouri.[3]

Coached by Herb Pailet, the New Orleans team held open tryouts at the local Young Men's Hebrew Association (YMHA) gym on Clio Street. Pailet was a New Orleans native and longtime executive with the Amateur Athletic Union (AAU) in the city. He had worked with the southern division of the NCAA basketball tournament and had even coached a local city league team based at the YMHA. This resumé made him an obvious choice for coach and general manager of the city's first professional team. In October 1947, Pailet announced that he had signed two players from Temple University's NCAA tournament team of 1944. Norman Rosen was a 6-foot, 2-inch forward, and Albie Ingerman "stands 5 feet 8 ½ inches and [is] considered a set shot artist as well as a fine floor man." But the team was mostly a conglomeration of former college standouts and locals who had gained experience at Loyola, Tulane, or the New Orleans Athletic Club. The Hurricanes, as they were called, would play southern division teams from Atlanta, Birmingham, and Chattanooga, but also northern division clubs from Chicago and Grand Rapids, Louisville and Kansas City, Omaha and Oklahoma City, and Waterloo, Iowa, and St. Paul, Minnesota.[4]

After the first week of play, the New Orleans media seemed confident of the success of both team and league. "This is the first pro cage team to represent New Orleans in a national league," explained the *Times-Picayune*, "and some of the top ranking basketball players in the country are listed on the roster." The league planned a seventy-game schedule, and while it was "still too early to draw conclusions from the first week statistics," the paper was certain that "all of the 16 teams appear evenly matched." An average of less than ten points decided the first week's games. Advertisements announced the team's upcoming home opener with Tulsa by touting the Hurricanes' "array of All-American stars." The AAU canceled its games for that night to clear the schedule for local basketball fans. Pailet's team even invited "the Jax Girls, who won the national amateur softball championship for the third successive year," to be their guests at the home opener. The interested parties did whatever possible to make the game a happening.[5]

The Hurricanes played at the Coliseum Arena at North Roman and Conti Streets, home since 1922 to a variety of big-time wrestling and boxing matches. Jack Dempsey, Gene Tunney, Joe Louis, and Sugar Ray Robinson all fought in the Coliseum Arena. The November 11 contest between the Hurricanes and the Tulsa Oilers would be less auspicious, as the locals would lose a close game to the visitors, 50–46. Played on a Tuesday, the matchup with the Oilers was the Hurricanes' first home contest after a series of losses on the road to start the season. A second home game against Grand Rapids, Michigan, was scheduled for Saturday. But it would not take place. On Thursday, two days after the Hurricanes' home opener, the league "blew up today in a splash of red ink," losing "a reported $500,000, including promotional expenses, in operating less than a month." Attendance, explained league attorney James O. Brooks, "has not been up to expectations, and it is good business judgement to terminate the league before further financial deficits are incurred." Brooks explained that all players and coaches would now be considered free agents, an important turn of events for star players like the Gears' George Mikan. For everyone else, however, being a free agent probably meant finding a job outside of basketball. For New Orleans, the league's end meant that the city's first run at professional basketball had come to an end after little more than a week.[6]

The Atlanta Basketball Club took a large advertisement in the *Atlanta Constitution* to celebrate its inclusion in the new league. "IN THE MAJORS!

Atlanta Has Joined The Major Leagues," the ad rejoiced. "We feel it fitting that this city, which long has ranked as major league in population, major league in industry and business and major league in civic achievement, should have that classification in professional sports."[7] The *Constitution* proudly announced, "The Atlanta entry in the newly formed Professional Basketball League of America will play 30 home games here at the Sports Arena court." A contest against rival Birmingham would begin the season, and road games "extending from New Orleans to St. Paul" would follow. The team's player-coach would be Coulby Gunther, a former star with St. John's University. Gunther had been lured from the Basketball Association of America with a two-year contract at $6,500 per year.[8]

The team featured a host of players who, like their coach, were decidedly unsouthern. Bob Fitzgerald and Mike McCarron played for Seton Hall. Center Bill Roberts starred at the University of Wyoming, and Howie Rader played at Long Island University. Rader's brother Len played for Birmingham, and Birmingham's seven-foot center, Elmore Morganthaler, starred at Boston College. Meanwhile, Chattanooga's player-coach was Henry "Dutch" Denhert, former center for the New York Celtics and coach of the Basketball Association of America's Cleveland Rebels. It was clear that southern teams like Atlanta, Chattanooga, and Birmingham (and unlike New Orleans, which staffed its team predominantly with locals) felt no need to litter their rosters with native talent if the entire playing pool was lily white.[9]

Also unlike New Orleans, Atlanta started its nascent season with seven straight victories. In its seventh, the team demonstrated the rough play that could be a hallmark of start-up professional basketball. "Two players, Harry Roberts, of Atlanta, and Dan Kirkland, the former University of Georgia star, were banished from the game in the second quarter for mixing it up a little too vigorously with elbows and fists," the *Constitution* reported. "Howie Rader, star Atlanta guard, also was sent to the showers when he pushed Referee Hymie Kaufman after the latter had called a foul against him."[10]

Such was the norm. The *Constitution* celebrated such fiascoes as part of the game's draw. In the team's first home game against Birmingham, for example, the paper thrilled as "Elmore Morganthaler and Harry Shor were ousted for flagrant fouls adding to the excitement in general. The Birmingham team hurled balls and jackets from the bench to further enliven the melee."[11] In its last game as a professional squad, and its only loss, the Atlanta team played Chattanooga in Chattanooga. Gunther complained about the officiating so profusely during the last five minutes of play that the referee called six straight technical fouls on him with one second remaining on the clock in a two-point game. Mike McCarron was so upset that he "grabbed the ball from the Chattanooga man out-of-bounds and drop-kicked it into the air." At that point, "a brawl broke out between the two teams following this incident and the police had to take a hand."[12]

They would not have to take a hand for long. James O. Brooks, an attorney for Commercial Sports Advertisers, the Professional Basketball League of America's parent company, explained in November 1947 that "the league attendance has been financially unsuccessful" and that it was forced to close. Atlanta's players were left just as frustrated as those in New Orleans.[13]

The *Atlanta Constitution* described the athletes as "dazed and undecided on their futures." Gunther's initial plan was to move the team "to some Eastern or Midwestern city where it could play an independent schedule." He felt betrayed. League officials had assured him that the endeavor had "ample backing. The promoters said they expected to lose money the first two years in order to get the league under way." In addition, Gunther doubted the claim of indigence, as per his understanding nine of the league's sixteen teams were in the black. He believed instead that "internal trouble at league headquarters" had caused the collapse. Meanwhile, Lamar Wells, manager of the Sports Arena, the team's titular home stadium, feared his own collapse if the team could not pay the rent for which it had originally signed. Making things more complicated, Gunther, Rader, McCarron, and another player, Harry Miller, were banned from the two other professional leagues, the Basketball Association of America and the National Basketball League, for jumping to the new group. As a result, their options were drastically limited. Gunter entered talks with Claire Bee, his former coach at Long Island University, to intercede with the BAA and have the ban lifted. The

Atlanta and Birmingham franchises agreed to play two additional games, one in each home city, to raise funds to help the players return home.[14]

This inauspicious start to professional basketball in the region wasn't the only start. During the 1947 season, the South also developed its own professional basketball circuit, the Southern Basketball League. It was the brainchild of *Nashville Tennessean* sports editor Raymond Johnson, who also served as league commissioner. The league placed teams in Jackson, Mississippi; Nashville and Memphis, Tennessee; and Birmingham, Montgomery, and Gadsden, Alabama.[15] Johnson, however, did not use his newspaper to promote his association, an expected synergy when sports editors typically became sports magnates. For example, his column on the day of the league's announcement concerned his SEC football predictions. The *Tennessean* relied on Associated Press coverage of the of league's founding despite the fact that the syndicated article quoted Johnson. Throughout the following week in September 1947, Johnson used his daily column to prepare his readers for college football. He never so much as mentioned the Southern Basketball League.[16]

Despite its upstart status, its founding newspaper's silence, and its competition from other organizations around the country, the league managed to be a draw for certain players. Birmingham's player-coach was Kevin "Chuck" Connors, for example, an all-around multisport athlete who starred for the Mobile Bears in baseball's Southern League and typically played in his off-season for the Boston Celtics. Connors abandoned the Celtics in 1947 for his newfound home-state professional team.[17]

And so the group muddled through that inaugural effort and, with the exception of certain teams, survived for another season in 1948. The league endured despite the continued sparse coverage by southern hometown newspapers. For instance, even after college football season, Johnson's sports section covered Vanderbilt's basketball team in far greater detail than his hometown professional squad. In December, Nashville was undefeated and the first-place team in the new league. Yet the *Tennessean* minimized coverage of Nashville's game against the Memphis Legionnaires in favor of accounts of Vanderbilt's upcoming road trip to play Mississippi State and Ole Miss. When reporting basketball scores around the region, the paper always listed collegiate and high school games before games of the "Southern Pro League." Momentum would always be somewhat stunted if even the league's founding newspaper paid such slight attention to its progress.[18]

With the success of Nashville's team, the league's founding newspaper would discover more enthusiasm for professional basketball during the March 1948 playoffs. "Nashville's Vols, winners of third place in the Southern Basketball league's regular season play, are practicing this week for their opening game of the playoffs," the *Tennessean* reported. It then rehearsed the team's roster and its prospects for the playoff. The plan had originally been for the top four teams to play, but second-place Jackson had too many injuries and bowed out of the postseason. First-place Montgomery and fourth-place Birmingham remained, along with Nashville. After the Volunteers defeated the Vulcans, the championship series left Nashville to face the regular season champions. The Montgomery Rebels had only lost six games throughout the regular season, and though the Vols were able to take the first game of the series, Montgomery won the rest. The *Tennessean*'s coverage was effusive after the first win. But it steadily dwindled after each additional loss, until the paper's reporting on the league championship was one small paragraph. This sort of coverage did not portend a bright future for the league.[19]

During that first year, the Memphis Legionnaires moved to Mobile, Alabama, becoming the Mobile Bears. The Gadsden, Alabama, Whiz Kids had to move as well, becoming the Bessemer Whiz Kids. Neither the Bears nor the Whiz Kids were able to survive into the league's second season. Nor were the Jackson Senators. Teams in Laurel, Mississippi, and New Orleans replaced the Mobile and Jackson franchises in that second season. The Laurel Oilers and the New Orleans Sports would meet in the season's opener in Mississippi in late November, beginning a short forty-game schedule that would last until late February.[20]

The Sports featured several Hurricane holdovers, including coach Herb Pailet. The team also included at least five Loyola alums, as well as Alex "Greek" Athas from Tulane, Sterling Scott from Valparaiso, and Bill Dwyer from Seton Hall. After losing their opener in Laurel, the Sports returned to the new John P. Lyons Memorial Center at Louisiana and Tchoupitoulas Streets for a home opener against Nashville. The Lyons Center, essentially a recreation center, was not the showcase that was Coliseum Arena. Its use demonstrated the more modest expectations of the new group.[21]

Still, Lyons could seat up to five thousand people if necessary, and the team was clearly a for-profit endeavor. It was the brainchild of Pailet and David Gertler, united as Sports Incorporated, which the *Times-Picayune* called a "group of business men who are interested in sport activities." An advocacy group devoted to bringing professional athletics to New Orleans, Sports Incorporated remained unfazed by the previous year's disaster. The local basketball team won that first home game. But its next matchup moved to the Westside Gym in Algiers for the Knights of Columbus's annual "Carnival of Sports" program for the city's West Side. The New Orleans Sports then returned to Lyons as its season-long home court.[22]

The stability of a home court was an important arbiter of legitimacy for the Sports, who normally received local press coverage below the fold. The team won and lost, won and lost throughout December and January, but attendance at Lyons Memorial remained sparse. Thus, in late January, "the New York Cover Girls, composed of the East's leading female cage performers," arrived at Lyons to face the Sports in an intergender exhibition. In early February, the New Orleans team took on the All-American Red Heads, featuring Gene Love, "the world's tallest woman performer who stands six feet four inches." The Red Heads, like the Cover Girls, barnstormed around the country playing men's teams in exhibitions. "All of the girls are expert at palming a basketball with one hand," the *Times-Picayune* reported, "and entertain crowds with trick stuff such as their 'baseball play,' under legs dribble, piggy back scores, fingertip ball spinning and a dancing dribbler." The game was designed to be a spectacle, a necessity in a city far more comfortable with spectacle than professional basketball.[23]

While the Sports were able to edge the Red Heads by three points, the contest would be the last in Lyons Memorial. The team lost regularly and was firmly in last place in the Southern Basketball League. Its most memorable moment was being on the losing end of a thirty-point drubbing by the eventual champion, the Montgomery Rebels. This contest featured a forty-one-point performance by Rebel guard Bobby Lowther. Poor play and dwindling attendance moved the Sports to the St. Aloysius school gymnasium at Esplanade and North Rampart Streets for the rest of the month. They closed the season there, managing a win total of only seven games. The league did not fare much better, canceling its postseason tournament and closing its doors at the end of the regular season.[24]

The Southern Basketball League's second season took place in a post–Jackie Robinson sports world. White supremacy prevailed in the postwar South, keeping the league's racial purity from becoming an issue with its predominantly white fans. Yet that insistence on racial purity would increasingly become a problem for southern sports in general. For instance, New Orleans's infamous segregation policy would affect its ability to draw athletes and athletics in the decades following World War II. In 1956, the NAACP petitioned the United States Military Academy's famed football team to cancel its game against Tulane because Louisiana law would segregate black military personnel at the stadium.[25]

Three years later, college basketball powerhouse Duquesne publicly rejected an offer to play in the annual Sugar Bowl basketball tournament held in conjunction with the city's major football bowl game. The school cited New Orleans's segregation practice as its reason for staying home. Such laws also limited Sugar Bowl organizers' choice of football teams for the bowl game. "Louisiana's segregation laws concerning sporting events," admitted one frustrated bowl official, "does present a problem in the selection of teams." Historian Kurt Edward Kemper argues that "no part of the South" took athletic segregation "as seriously as the state of Louisiana."[26] Moreover, the laws presented a problem in the recruitment of professionals. And so the following year, in February 1960, the state sports segregation law mandating separate competition fell to pragmatism, as Loyola New Orleans hosted integrated Loyola Chicago in a basketball game. The contest took place at Loyola Field House, the future home of the city's first integrated professional team.[27]

Birmingham's relationship with integrated sports was even more fraught. From 1948 to 1951, the Birmingham Junior Chamber of Commerce hosted a charity NFL game each season. In 1950, the Detroit Lions' Wally Triplett was forced to sit on the bench in the team's Birmingham game against Washington. The following season, two New York Giants were barred from playing, leading to the cancelation of the game. Conflict led the city to formalize such practices. A special sports segregation ordinance declared, "It shall be unlawful for a Negro and a white person to play together or in company with each other in any game." In 1953, in response to the city edict, Harvard University's track-and-field team withdrew from the Southern Relays held at Legion Field.[28]

In February 1954, the year after Harvard's absence, the Birmingham City Commission voted to eliminate segregation in the playing of football and baseball. This measure responded directly to the NFL scandals and the fact that baseball's Atlanta Crackers, members of the same Southern League as the Birmingham Barons, included three black players and would inevitably have to play in the city. The Associated Negro Press speculated on a different reason for the vote: "It could be that Eugene (Bull) Connor, known for his anti-Negro tirades, no longer is a member of the City Commission." Regardless of the reason, this was an unquestionably positive development. Yet it did not include basketball (or softball, dominoes, checkers, or other parlor games, for that matter). The commission simply removed baseball and football from the list of segregated sports, leaving basketball in the category of card games and dice.[29] White Birmingham seemed reluctantly on board with the decision until the Supreme Court's *Brown v. Board of Education* decision in May. The ruling prompted a public referendum that not only revoked the commission's integration move but also strengthened audience segregation in public gatherings like sporting events. Such tactics were part of the city's comprehensive resistance to *Brown*.[30]

Thus when black professional basketball teams the Harlem Magicians and the New York Olympians scheduled a game in Birmingham in January 1957, the requirement that white and black audiences had to attend separately drew protests. The Birmingham Baptist Ministers Conference and organizations like the Alabama Christian Movement for Human Rights and the Emancipation Association of Birmingham petitioned promoters to cancel the game unless everyone could attend the same contest.[31] The petitions went unheeded, and separate games were played, much to the dismay of many black residents of the region. One letter writer from Tuscaloosa pointed out that four black churches and two ministers' homes had recently been bombed "because of their fight against segregation." "I am sure if these outstanding athletes knew that Negroes are now making great sacrifices for first-class citizenship," the correspondent explained, "they would not come South to stamp their approval on segregation by playing to segregated groups."[32]

And then there was Georgia. In 1957, the legislature narrowly failed to pass a new sports segregation law that prohibited any integrated competition in the state. It began another effort to revive the attempt in 1958. A frustrated Marion Jackson, sports editor of the *Atlanta Daily World*, argued, "The white folks of Georgia are willing to surrender their civil liberties in obedience to the idol god of jimcrow rather than to take a stand for decency and tolerance." He pointed out that southern legislatures had passed no legislation beneficial to black residents following the *Brown* decision. Jackson also noted that new segregation laws like Georgia's sports effort still proliferated, even though they were cutting off the state's nose to spite its face by prohibiting both good competition and legitimate revenue.[33]

In 1961, seven black men were arrested in Savannah after playing basketball on a municipal court reserved for whites. The Georgia NAACP, which was monitoring the case, claimed that it was impossible to tell whether the action was intended as a protest because the city did not have any municipal courts that were not designated for whites.[34] In 1962, to Savannah's north in Atlanta, Georgia Tech announced that it would resume a formerly canceled football series with the United States Naval Academy in 1964. The series originally ended because the academy would not participate in a game wherein players or spectators were segregated. Its resumption was a bellwether of coming changes to segregated sports in Atlanta through the mid-1960s.[35]

Still, if a relaxation of racial restrictions existed for football and baseball, it was the maintenance of such restrictions that colored the black South's response to professional basketball. The bulk of basketball coverage in the *Atlanta Daily World*, the South's largest black newspaper and the hub of a syndicate that spread throughout the region, emphasized black collegiate basketball in the Southern Intercollegiate Athletic Conference. Teams from Atlanta schools like Morehouse, Clark, and Morris Brown merited particular attention. There was always an eye, however, on the black professionals in the north. The New York Renaissance Five took the 1939 championship by winning the first annual World Professional Basketball Tournament, and the Harlem Globetrotters won the title the following year. The Chicago *Herald American* sponsored the tournament, and over the course of its existence from 1939 to 1948, its winner was generally considered the world champion of basketball. After the Rens and Globetrotters, integrated teams like the Detroit Eagles, the Oshkosh Stars, and the Washington Bears claimed this title. The Ft. Wayne Zollner Pistons followed with a three-year championship run from 1944 to 1946.[36]

The *World* kept tabs on such contests, though they all featured northern teams. Like so many others, the paper was particularly infatuated with black teams like the New York Rens and the Chicago-based Harlem Globetrotters. However, the black southern press uniformly ignored the region's lily-white professional teams when they came into existence in 1947. Locality only mattered when coupled with racial inclusion. Until southern professional teams with black players as either part or all of the roster became a reality, professional basketball in all of its forms would remain tertiary for the black southern population.[37]

By March and April, the time of the World Professional Basketball Tournament, the *Louisiana Weekly*, New Orleans's black newspaper, had largely moved on to coverage of baseball. It made no mention of the annual championship after white teams like Ft. Wayne began taking the title. Yet the paper provided a wealth of local basketball coverage and a weekly column during the season called "Swish! Two Points!!" that covered all levels of competition.[38] "Basketball is [one of] the nation's top sports," the *Atlanta Daily World* reported. "No sport approaches it in mass appeal." People loved the game because it was fast paced and filled with action. As the paper stated, "Basketball boasts more storybook finishes than a Horatio Alger novel. For lightning-gated, whiz-bang, hardwood necromancy no indoor sport matches it." On top of that, it was inexpensive and in many places easily accessible, but the "biggest handicap to basketball is the lack of facilities.

This is especially true in the South where facilities for play and spectators are almost non-existent."[39]

Such racial inconsistencies also existed at the national level. As Damion L. Thomas notes, in the decade following World War II, the State Department "attempted to develop a relationship" with the Harlem Globetrotters, hoping to encourage black Americans to see the American Dream as "available to individual African Americans despite segregation." The State Department did so, Thomas argues, because it saw "the Globetrotters' cooning as well as their degrading caricatures of African Americans" as reflecting "the behavior, attitudes, and mind-set of most black Americans. Hence, State Department arguments simultaneously stressed racial progress, but also the notion that African Americans' 'unsophisticated behavior' made them unfit or at least ill-prepared for full equality." This situation led even black basketball success to work against integration, against the full participation of black players with white. As the federal government sponsored this state of affairs, owners' later racial concerns were understandable, if not a fait accompli.[40]

Meanwhile, the decidedly nonsouthern National Basketball Association struggled with its own racial inconsistencies. The *Pittsburgh Courier*'s Jack Saunders, for example, took the Philadelphia Warriors to task in 1953 for being one of the last professional basketball holdouts in hiring black players. "Apparently the Philadelphia Warriors have too many good white players to give Negro players a break," wrote Saunders facetiously. The hiring restrictions remained in place despite the fact that "the Warriors had lost 27 of 33 games played." There were many who accused the team of prejudice. Saunders further stated, "If that be true the owners of the Warriors think more of prejudice than they think of money." The paper cast most of the blame on Eddie Gottlieb, the Warriors' owner and coach, who was rumored to consider quitting because of the team's lack of success. Saunders argued that this situation could have been avoided by incorporating talented black players.[41]

"Has the National Basketball Association the strength to protect its players from segregation practices in biased cities?" asked *World* sports editor Marion Jackson. The answer, as of February 1959, seemed to be yes. In response to segregation in West Virginia, Minneapolis Lakers star forward Elgin Baylor refused to play in an exhibition game. "A pro basketball player dunked a free throw through the hoop of segregation," proclaimed the *Los Angeles Sentinel* in a confused metaphor. When Baylor's Lakers were scheduled to play Cincinnati in Charleston, the city assured Minneapolis president Bob Short that the team would encounter no segregation. Even so, the local hotel refused to accommodate Baylor and his black teammates. The entire team moved to a black hotel, and Baylor refused to participate in the game. "Such is the stuff men are made of," gushed the *Sentinel*.[42]

A local promoter for the American Business Club, which sponsored the Charleston game, demanded that the NBA punish its young star for not playing. But the association defended Baylor and responded to the incident with a staunch antisegregation policy. Association president Maurice Podoloff announced that before any NBA team played in a nonleague city, "we will insist on a clause to protect players and clubs from embarrassment." The Lakers agreed. Short announced that the team would play no further neutral-site games "unless we are guaranteed common facilities for rooming and feeding all our players." The *Sentinel* praised Short as well, but Baylor was the story. His "refusal to compromise with all the evil that segregation stands for is a tribute to his character and should give the fainthearted something to think about. He has shown the way."[43]

Baylor's actions "will do much to topple ole Jim Crow from the sports picture," guessed black press columnist Brock Brockenbury. "This was an act that even Jackie Robinson might have hesitated to pull." Such was a common theme of newspapers' coverage of the Charleston incident. Columnist Dan Burley claimed that Baylor "overnight has become the 'Jackie Robinson' of pro basketball in his strictly one-man crusade against southern Jim Crow." Brockenbury encouraged his readers to send letters of thanks to both Baylor and the Lakers to assure officials that "what they did is appreciated by us."[44] Baylor was grateful for the support. "I've appreciated the many replies I've received from various parts of the country," he announced. "I want it understood, however, that I didn't take this stand to become a hero. I just felt it wasn't right for me to play in a town where I couldn't be treated on an equal basis with the rest of the team."[45]

While Baylor's refusal to play was new, the segregated treatment of NBA teams was not. Just weeks prior to the West Virginia fiasco, in December 1958, a similar incident occurred when the Lakers played the Boston Celtics in Charlotte, North Carolina. Black players for both teams, including Baylor and Bill Russell, were forced to eat at different restaurants and stay in different lodgings than their white teammates. Both played in the Charlotte game, but neither of them were happy. "I don't care if we ever go back," said an angry Walter Brown, owner of the Celtics. "I know one thing—I'll never do anything to embarrass my players." Robert Short was similarly upset, just as he would be again in February. It was after the Charlotte incident that Baylor told the team owner he would not play if a similar incident occurred.[46]

Though Russell had not been in Charleston for Baylor's refusal to play, he supported him unequivocally. "Elgin didn't do what he did for himself alone," he told the *New York Post*. "He did it for me and every other Negro player in the league." Russell described his own similar experiences in junior college and on the Olympic team. "This is a white man's world," he explained. "They take us and they educate us. They say: 'You're going to help. Be on your best behavior.' They give us their religion, their code of ethics, their way to dress and to live and then they don't live up to it." It was high-order betrayal. "They draw a line and we're not supposed to go over it. What do you think it does to a person inside? Do you think you ever get over it?"[47] With such treatment, and the mistreated players' justifiable anger, the notion of continued professional games in the South was far-fetched, to say nothing of permanent NBA residency.

Even on professional teams with liberal management and general rapport between black and white players, explained columnist Brock Brockenbury, "subtle prejudice pops up in little ways, in the conversation of the players, in their habits, in the little involuntary groupings and the like."[48] In 1962, just three years after the West Virginia incident, those continued problems led Bill Russell to announce that he planned to move to Africa after his playing career.[49] Russell experienced yet another indignity during the season, this time at a segregated restaurant in Lexington, Kentucky. After being refused service at a restaurant in the city, five Celtics players and two from the St.

Louis Hawks booked tickets on the next flight out of town and did not compete. "The people of Lexington, who had a double standard at that time, were not offended at the game that evening," wrote Russell. "They got just what they apparently wanted—a lily-white basketball game."[50]

While the manager of the hotel where the incident occurred called the fiasco a misunderstanding, Celtics coach Red Auerbach took the players to the airport himself. "I couldn't possibly order them to play," he said.[51] Around that same time, Oakland was scheduled to play an exhibition in Houston. As Russell explained, "The NAACP asked the Negro players to refuse to play under the segregated seating laws that were in force." There was no such request from the NAACP in Lexington, but a frustrated Russell served much the same function.[52]

College players faced similar conditions when they entered the South. Chet Walker, a Bradley University standout in 1960, described horrendous treatment when his Illinois team made a swing through the region. His coach told the black players "to expect racism and offensive treatment, that it was just the way things were and there was nothing he or we could do about it. Implicit was the idea that we better not cause any incident that would reflect badly on the team or on Bradley. The message was that the South was going to be different because we were different: this is your lot, accept it, don't make waves if you want to play."[53]

With such racial incidents mounting, the upstart American Basketball League (ABL)began play in 1961 without any southern teams, despite the fact that the South was absent NBA outfits. The new league, created by Harlem Globetrotters owner Abe Saperstein, instead put teams in non-NBA cities in the Northeast and far West, including one in Hawaii. In addition, the ABL directly challenged the association in Chicago and Los Angeles. The South might have been an untapped professional basketball market, but the ABL was a product of the Globetrotters' owner, and it would even be, among other things, the first professional league to feature black head coaches. The league's Pittsburgh franchise called itself the Rens, an homage to the legendary black team the Harlem Renaissance Five. As such, even Hawaii was less out-of-the-way than the South. The ABL collapsed in 1963 with roughly $2 million in losses. It couldn't compete with the NBA in the

West and Northeast, and it struggled with an unwieldy travel schedule that included Hawaii. A venture that seemed a signpost for future attempts, the ABL indicated that untapped markets like the South might be the best method of finding success.[54]

The *Pittsburgh Courier* announced in August 1963, just after the ABL's collapse, that professional basketball had "grown by leaps and bounds down through the years and Negro stars have grown with it." It described Elgin Baylor, Bill Russell, Wilt Chamberlain, and Oscar Robertson as the unquestioned leaders in the game.[55] What the *Courier* did not include in its celebration was the fact that NBA leadership perceived a roster of black stars as a drain on the league's popularity.[56]

That month, August 1963, the NBA Board of Governors held a series of meetings designed to dramatically improve the long-term health of the league. The association had played during the previous season without a television deal and had suffered as a consequence. At those meetings, the board replaced the association's original president, Maurice Podoloff. The new leader, former Harlem Globetrotters publicity director and mayor of Stamford, Connecticut, J. Walter Kennedy, initiated a platform of strict discipline to sanitize the NBA's reputation. "Few professional athletes ever bother to read their contracts," Kennedy explained, because there was "one specific line in their contract which gives me unusual power—the power to ban them from the NBA for life for conduct I feel detrimental to basketball." Players faced myriad new rules. They were told, for example, not to socialize with gamblers. "They have been told to check carefully before allowing their picture to be taken with people they don't know," said Kennedy. "And if any NBA players do get into trouble, they can expect no mercy from me." The new league president even fined Red Auerbach for not leaving the floor after receiving two technical fouls during a game.[57]

The board also expanded the maximum active roster from eleven to twelve team members, placing an extra uniformed player at the end of professional benches. With those changes, the association managed a new television contract for a Game of the Week beginning in January 1964. Podoloff, retired but seeing much progress in the league's alterations, also formed a committee to examine the possibility of expansion to ten teams the following season. The most curious aspect of such corporate maneuvering was the roster expansion. While all the other actions would increase revenues, adding athletes to teams would only limit them. Many people, including some of the NBA's black players, assumed that the association became less marketable as its talent became blacker. Thus roster expansion was a maneuver to add another white player to teams to make them more in demand.[58] "The NBA has apparently purged itself of the quota system," Bill Russell wrote in 1970, indicating his belief that though it lacked official documentation, such an arrangement clearly existed. "The day in 1965 that Red [Auerbach] started five blacks—and we went on to win the title—that was the end of the quota system."[59]

August 1963 was seminal for the NBA because of the association's Board of Governors meeting. But the month was better known for a different meeting, the March on Washington, which Elgin Baylor, along with more than 200,000 others, attended. That month also witnessed the announcement of Baylor's role as a Nigerian United Nations delegate in Bob Hope's new movie, *A Global Affair*. Thus, outside of the South, the NBA's concern about black stars was ultimately unnecessary.[60]

Baltimore Bullets rookie Gus Johnson, a black power forward from the University of Idaho who would eventually make the NBA's All-Rookie First Team, dominated that season. Black players routinely cited Johnson as an exemplar of the extra work it took for African Americans to succeed in basketball. The Akron high school standout was always overshadowed by Jerry Lucas, a white player from Middletown, in the southern part of the state. Lucas got a scholarship to Ohio State, while Johnson settled for Idaho. When the two got to the NBA, Johnson always made playing against Lucas a priority. "Gus eats him alive, and Jerry doesn't do much against Gus," said one player. "You can see Gus out there and I know he's thinking: 'I had nothing in my life, never had, and this big white kid had everything. I'll show him, I'll show him.'"[61]

It was Du Bois's double consciousness writ onto basketball gymnasiums around the country, and it could be motivating or utterly disheartening, depending on the player. "I consider my life up to the present time a waste," Bill Russell explained in April 1963. "I don't consider anything I've done as contributing to society." Playing basketball was "marking time, the most shallow thing in the world." Russell demonstrated an uncompromising frustration with race relations. "I accepted things I shouldn't have," he said. "Little things. Like the fact that a police car stopped every time it went by and a few of us were talking on the corner. I thought it stopped for everybody. Now I know it only stopped for US [capitalization Russell's]."[62]

In February 1966, *Sport Magazine* published one of its most controversial articles, an investigation into NBA executives' fears about race. Journalist John Devaney delved into what he called "pro basketball's hidden fear." The exposé began with a charged question by Howard Cosell to Wilt Chamberlain. "Are we reaching the point," Cosell asked in a WABC radio interview, "where perhaps there are too many Negro players in the National Basketball Association for box office appeal?" It was an intentionally provocative question from an intentionally provocative self-promoter, but Chamberlain's answer was even more surprising: "I definitely think that probably we have."[63]

Seven of the ten starters in the association's 1965 All-Star Game, for example, were black. "Nobody wants to say anything, but of course the owners are worried," admitted one NBA coach. "How are you going to draw with eleven colored players on your team?" While this was a worrisome question to many in the association, others found it ridiculous. All, however, agreed that the league was blackening. In the 1955–56 season, six of the NBA's eighty players were black. One of them, Maurice Stokes, made the All-Star Game. At the beginning of the 1965–66 season, the association had ninety-nine players, forty-seven of whom were black. Of that number, thirty-one were starters, and fourteen made the All-Star Game. Almost half the players, two-thirds of the starters, and three-quarters of the all-stars were African American. This was the racial makeup in a league where fans were close to the players, and where those players wore no hats or helmets, making themselves far more visible than athletes in any other professional league. In his exposé, Devaney also noted that the best collegiate players in every class were black, meaning that the trend would only continue.[64]

The problem, argued Devaney, was "race prejudice," and it was everywhere. "The fear of NBA owners, the question that worries them is: in a society that is 90 percent white, is this prejudice—this inability of some white spectators to identify with Negro athletes—deep enough and widespread enough to hold back NBA growth?" The answer of both NBA publicity director Haskell Cohen and league commissioner Walter Kennedy was an unqualified no. Both pointed to rising attendance over the same decade that included the rise of the black superstar. "When a team wins, it draws," Cohen explained. "When it loses, attendance falls off. It's as simple as that."[65]

The Boston Celtics' experience countered such claims. The Celtics had been champions for seven straight seasons, and the team's average attendance in the 1960–61 season was 7,448 per game. Four years later, the team averaged 8,779 fans per game. This number was, to be sure, an improvement, but the Celtics' arena held 13,909. In his interview with Cosell, Chamberlain chalked up such relative stagnation amid overwhelming success to the continued blackening of the team. White stars like Bob Cousy and Bill Sharman were being replaced with black stars like Sam Jones and K. C. Jones. "Why should a team with a record compiled such as it has not draw to capacity crowds," asked Chamberlain, "whereas the hockey team fills the house almost every night?"[66]

Another consideration was television, which accommodated viewers beyond the arena. ABC television paid the AFL $2 million for sixteen football games, and it paid the NBA $750,000 for seventeen basketball games. "In broadcasting circles," Devaney claimed, "it was said that the reason for the disparity in prices was the lack of a white NBA star." Of course, Walter Kennedy denied such claims, but he was not in the broadcasting business. ABC's ratings for professional basketball were not bad, but Devaney seemed onto something. "I'm only being realistic," a television executive told the reporter, "when I say that if a white center were to come along to challenge Chamberlain or Russell, the ratings for those games would jump fifty percent."[67]

One of the certain victims of the racial worry in the NBA was the black fringe player. One NBA official explained that "up to 1960 or so, you kept a colored player as your ninth or tenth man. You had to pay him only $6,500 or so, a lot less than you had to pay a white boy. But not anymore. Now the tenth and 11th players are white boys, to balance out the squad." Teams replaced white players with white players and black players with black players, keeping a racial consistency that would maintain fans' expectations. Myriad stories emerged of management telling team executives to draft white players to mollify a fan base, and of those executives ultimately missing out on black players who would become stars. The stories of marginal black players losing jobs at the end of an NBA team bench were myriad as well.[68]

According to rumors, such was the reason rosters had expanded to eleven players in 1963. "Times have changed—for the better—but prejudice did not die with the Civil Rights Act of 1964," wrote Devaney. "The NBA knows it is facing a problem." Expansion again seemed to be a solution, but this time with more teams, rather than more players on the end of the bench. "The thinking is that at least 50 percent of these new jobs would be filled by Negroes, but others would be taken by whites who otherwise would be shut out of the NBA." In addition, expansion would allow the association to divide into four divisions, "giving better balance and more winners. And winners usually do well at the box office."[69]

The suggestion of expansion, of course, portended a move to the Deep South. Both New Orleans and Atlanta had applied for new franchises, and the prospects for a move seemed good by the mid-1960s. The St. Louis Hawks, a team "with seven Negroes on the squad," scheduled eight of its games in the 1965–66 season in Memphis. Attendance at those games averaged a respectable 7,501 fans. "An NBA club would go over in the South with 50 percent Negro players," a white southern player explained, "but the team would have to be a winner." It was a curious assessment, at once ominous and optimistic.[70]

Devaney's exposé turned out to be, in the words of a *Sport Magazine* writer, "one of the most controversial stories we have ever run." The publication was inundated with mail parsing every conceivable issue related to race and professional basketball, but *Sport* vigorously stood by its story. "We heard that there was a fear, an anxiety, among the powerbrokers of the NBA," the magazine wrote several months later, "that pro basketball wasn't growing the way it should because there were too many Negroes in the league." The Devaney investigation had proven such rumors true.

"He found out that some people in the NBA felt that the preponderance of Negro players was hurting the gate. He found out that some people feared an almost-total takeover of the NBA by Negroes."[71]

While the NBA's fear was real, so too was its potential for expansion. Many opportunistic entrepreneurs saw southern cities as ripe for professional basketball. When the American Basketball Association arrived the year following *Sport*'s race investigation to challenge the hegemony of the NBA, it followed in the footsteps of other rival upstarts like the American Football League, expressly intent on challenging the established association and forcing a merger. The ABA sought to put teams in new, emerging markets so that they could be successful without directly competing with the established league. In so doing, it hoped to demonstrate viability and make a merger more likely. The South provided all of the criteria, and so the new association included teams in New Orleans, Dallas, Houston, and Louisville for its inaugural 1967–68 season. Only the New Orleans Buccaneers played in a traditional Deep South market that season. Yet the ABA demonstrated that there could be at least marginal success on the region's periphery.[72]

And what success existed was certainly marginal. The Houston ABA franchise struggled in its first season, once drawing only eighty-nine fans to a game. A frustrated T. C. Morrow, Houston's owner, dropped out of the association, and a group of investors brought the team to North Carolina for the 1968–69 season. ABA audiences in Dallas were shocked by coaches' foul language and players' fights. "These were gentlemen," remembered Terry Stembridge, the Chaparrals' radio announcer, "and they came to a nice Sunday afternoon basketball game with their kids." The struggles of the team in New Orleans were even more difficult, rivaling the city's unsuccessful stints with the Hurricanes and the Sports in the 1940s. The ABA listed its first-year attendance at 1,200,439, an average of just under 3,000 fans per game. Historian Terry Pluto refers to such numbers as "wildly overstated." Indiana and Denver led the league in average attendance at 6,000 and 4,000, respectively. The southern teams remained at the bottom of attendance lists and the bottom of the league standings.[73]

New Orleans's experience with the ABA was fundamentally different than its brief early experiences on the fringes of professional basketball. The ABA was unique. It was brash. But it was not on the fringe. And unlike previous attempts at professional basketball in the South, the ABA was integrated. In fact, black players dominated the league. When New Orleans found itself with a team in the NBA's upstart rival, the event marked the arrival of major-league integrated professional basketball to the Deep South. It would establish precedents that the region would follow for the next decade.

2

THE TALK-SHOW HOST IN NEW ORLEANS

Morton Downey Jr. and his wife Joan were eating at a New Orleans restaurant in 1967 when an acquaintance approached and asked the beautiful woman about her mother being Burmese. When Joan Downey confirmed her mother's heritage, the acquaintance replied that "you don't have any oriental features at all." The acquaintance then turned to Joan's husband and asked, "Did you ever notice any oriental characteristics in your wife?" Morton Downey thought for a moment and said, "Only when she irons my shirts."[1]

That kind of casual bigotry would make Downey a celebrity in the 1980s, when he became a progenitor of right-wing talk television. But in the 1960s his career and its trajectory took a very different turn. Downey lived in New Orleans for fewer than two years, arriving in early 1966 and leaving in late 1967, but he had a substantial impact on the city. During this short period, he would become the driving force behind the creation of the American Basketball Association's New Orleans Buccaneers. Despite his later demagoguery, he would also ensure that the team's original incarnation developed without concern for the racist whims of its potential fans. Such was not the case in nearby Atlanta when that city adopted the NBA's Hawks in 1968. While Downey was a carpetbagging northerner, his civic activism would ultimately develop the Crescent City's professional sports reputation and lay the groundwork for its future basketball endeavors. Precisely because Downey was a carpetbagging northerner, he would do so largely without regard to race.

While New Orleans was undergoing its early failed attempts at professional basketball under Herb Paillet and the New Orleans Sports, Downey was living the life of a wealthy, privileged teenager. Born in 1932 to famed tenor Morton Downey, the younger Downey grew up in affluent Hyannis Port, Massachusetts. A neighbor of the Kennedy family, he played regularly with Jack and Bobby and Teddy in their front yard. Downey attended New York University but dropped out to pursue a career as a singer and songwriter, the beginning of what *Time* magazine called an "eclectic, not to say bizarre, career."[2]

Downey had several hit songs in his music career, most notably recording "Boulevard of Broken Dreams" in 1957. In the late 1950s he signed with Memphis's Stax Records. Almost all of his fellow musicians at the company were black. While touring through the South, Downey and Fats Domino entered a Tuscaloosa, Alabama, restaurant where an employee told them, "We don't serve niggers here." Without hesitation, Domino replied, "I don't want a nigger. I want a hamburger." Downey stormed out of the restaurant and credited the incident with "the beginnings of a realization that I had to work with my friends to bring about change." He participated in civil rights marches throughout the South, never leading, but taking part nonetheless. It was in the movement that he befriended Jesse Jackson, to whom he would remain close for the rest of his life.[3]

While singing and songwriting, Downey also served as a disc jockey in Chicago, Los Angeles, and Miami, but he decided that he needed a more stable career. "If you don't make it big by 35 as a writer," he explained, "it's time to get out. And if you don't make it by 25 as a singer, get out." So he took a job as general manager of catering and vending machine conglomerate Canteen Corporation's Louisiana division in early 1966. It was not a glamorous position, hardly matching that of recording star and DJ. Later that year, a combination of adventure and civic pride led Downey to help create New Orleans Pro Basketball Associates (NOPBA), a booster organization designed to bring an NBA team to the city. The organization was founded on December 20 with the goal of obtaining an expansion franchise in the league for $1.5 million.[4]

Two weeks later, however, Downey was negotiating directly with St. Louis Hawks owner Ben Kerner about selling the team to the group and bringing it to New Orleans. "I went to St. Louis with the impression that we didn't have a chance of getting the team," said Downey, but "I figured the trip would be worth it anyway. The contacts would have been extremely valuable and our group felt obligated to New Orleans." Yet negotiations progressed quickly. "To give you an idea of how fast things happened," he explained, "my wife didn't know what had transpired until I came home. I got off the plane and she asked 'How'd it go?' and I replied, 'I just bought us a basketball team.'" Ultimately, Downey made a $3.8 million offer, more than twice the cost of the original expansion team plan. "I would like to keep the team in St. Louis," said Kerner. "But unless the New Orleans price is matched by the deadline I must sell to New Orleans."[5]

Downey traveled to St. Louis with legal counsel Steve R. Plotkin and with his second-in-command, association vice president Jules Kimble. "All of a sudden the Saints may have company," wrote the New Orleans *States-Item*'s Peter Finney. "Would you believe the New Orleans Hawks?" He reported that "a local pro basketball group, headed by a frustrated dribbler named Sean Morton Downey, reached a tentative agreement" to buy the Hawks. Downey did his best to dispel reporters' doubts, claiming that the expense was worth the reward, and that the team was bound to be a success in New Orleans. "We plan to put on a show, something besides basketball," he told Finney. "You can look for halftime entertainment with stars like Barbra Streisand and Robert Goulet." Finney, however, was skeptical. "What—No Frank Sinatra?" he asked his readers, tongue in cheek. "For the championship playoffs, maybe."[6]

Upon returning to New Orleans, however, Kimble pulled out of the group in an obvious attempt to sabotage the deal. Kimble told the St. Louis *Post-Dispatch* that he was prepared to invest half of the $3.8 million price tag for the team, but Downey and his colleagues noted that his actual share was only $150,000. Kimble claimed to be dropping out because "there were several persons in the 13-man group with whom he did not want to be associated," reported the *Post-Dispatch*. "He said that he had not been aware of their identities when he first committed his money to the syndicate." Downey downplayed Kimble's absence, but the two men were the New Orleans representatives who signed the original agreement with St. Louis. Unfortunately, Kimble had claimed to have $1.5 million, but, according to Downey, he had "misrepresented his worth by $1,499,999.99." After the debacle, WWL's sports director Hap Glaudi investigated and found that Kimble was an oil rig worker.[7]

This would not be Kimble's first involvement in fraud and controversy. He was a longtime ranking member in Louisiana's Ku Klux Klan, and in July 1967, just a few months after his negotiations with Downey for the Hawks, he would be implicated in two home bombings in Baton Rouge. Kimble would also do his best to place himself in the John F. Kennedy assassination controversy by claiming different versions of nefarious relationships with David Ferrie, Guy Bannister, and Clay Shaw in New Orleans. Later, Kimble claimed that he was once a CIA handler for James Earl Ray in Canada, and that he was ultimately part of a government conspiracy to assassinate Martin Luther King. In 1976, Kimble and his brother would be convicted on federal racketeering and murder charges and sentenced to life imprisonment. Such was not the typical profile of a civic leader and basketball booster.[8]

Those larger frauds, however, would come later. Kimble's misrepresentation of his wealth in the St. Louis negotiations had not completely soured the potential deal. "Downey insists that his only goal is to acquire a professional basketball franchise for the city. When it does get here," reported the *Times-Picayune*'s Will Peneguy, "he won't necessarily figure in the ownership structure." But Downey didn't have to; he was "basketball's answer to Dave Dixon." It was high praise. Dixon was the civic booster vital to bringing the New Orleans Saints and the Superdome to the city, and he was pleased with Downey's effort. NOPBA was meeting with Loyola about using the school's field house. Even so, Dixon suggested that the team use the Rivergate, the Port of New Orleans exhibition center, which was then completing construction. He recommended loaning the team the portable seats for the new dome to be constructed at the Rivergate. "It would give the facility a seating capacity of approximately 8,000," Dixon explained, "and when the domed stadium is completed the stands can be returned."[9]

Unlike Dixon, however, Downey had only been in New Orleans since 1966, and he did not have $3.8 million. "We wanted to use only Louisiana money," said Downey, "but that plan didn't materialize." The initial plan was to play most Hawks home games at the Rivergate. But nine would be played in Memphis, five in Shreveport, and an undetermined number in Louisville. With that plan in place, Downey arranged a flight to St. Louis with local judge David Gertler and attorney Steven Plotkin, both part of the NOPBA, to make a $100,000 down payment on the team. "There are numerous things to iron out concerning the franchise," Downey explained. "It now looks as if the Hawks will be in New Orleans in 1967."[10]

Downey, however, did not go to St. Louis, and the Hawks did not come to New Orleans. Irving Roth replaced Downey on the trip, and the three more fiscally responsible parties realized that $3.8 million was a near-impossible ask. They lowered the offer, and Kerner rejected it. Gertler, serving as spokesman for the group, claimed that the reduced offer was not the result of an inability to pay, but he also declined to provide any other reason. He claimed that the door hadn't officially closed on purchasing the Hawks, and if even if it had, "We will continue our efforts to seek a basketball franchise for this city as soon as possible." This vague and unedifying pronouncement did little to explain why the St. Louis deal fell through. *Picayune* sports editor Bob Roesler had mixed feelings about the collapse. "I'm not excited by the NBA brand of basketball. You know, shoot, shoot, run, run. To me if you watch the last five minutes of a pro game, you'll see enough," he claimed. "Yet, I must admit, I felt bad when Downey's combine and the Kerner forces ruptured contract talks. Maybe the sport would have gone over here. Right now it looks like we'll never know the answer. Not for awhile."[11]

"Awhile," however, would be a shorter period of time than Roesler expected. Less than a week after the failed St. Louis deal, Downey flew to Los Angeles to meet with a group forming the American Basketball Association. Then he flew to New York for another series of meetings at the St. Regis Hotel. His negotiations with the ABA were far more successful, and on January 22 the league approved a new franchise for New Orleans at the reduced price of

$260,000. "All anyone had to do to get a franchise was to say he had money," remembered Gary Davidson, one of the league's founders, "to appear to have money, and to say he wanted a franchise and was prepared to support one until it succeeded." If nothing else, Downey's group fit that bill. The new franchise was a consolation prize, but a prize nonetheless. "New Orleans will have a professional basketball team next season after all," wrote the *States-Item*'s Nat Belloni. Downey promised the same kind of star-filled halftime entertainment as he had for the Hawks.[12]

The ABA was founded when Southern California promoter Dennis Murphy failed in a venture to get an American Football League (AFL) franchise for Anaheim in 1965. The AFL and NFL merged that year, ending his hope for a football team. Murphy then decided to parlay the group he had assembled for that effort and create a basketball league to compete with the NBA. With only twelve teams in the established group for 1966, the creation of a rival league might facilitate a merger similar to that happening in football. From there, investment, promotion, and sports people began to come onboard. George Mikan's arrival as commissioner was the last step prior to the press conference in New York announcing the creation of the ABA. There would be a three-point shot. The ball would be red, white, and blue. "We had no plan," Indiana's Dick Tinkham said of the ABA's formation. "Sure, we wanted to merge with the NBA. That was a goal. But a plan? We had none. We went by the seat of our pants and made it up as we went along."[13]

Organizers wanted to rival the NBA and encourage a merger, so they worked to bring professional basketball to cities that did not already have NBA franchises. The South fit that bill. Despite its reluctance to go to the Deep South, the ABA did place teams in Dallas, Houston, Louisville, and New Orleans. Even with that strategy, however, the league unapologetically identified itself racially. The NBA had black stars like Wilt Chamberlain and Bill Russell but had struggled with race and its relationship to fans. The NBA hadn't included black players until 1951, and their further inclusion was restricted to a slow trickle throughout the 1950s. In contrast, the ABA actively pursued black athletes. As historian James Whiteside notes, the league was founded "in the immediate wake of the most active and successful period of America's civil rights struggle." The league also wanted a more flamboyant, less fundamental style that officials believed black athletes could provide. Just as the ABA would play in different cities than the NBA, it would attempt to play to a different audience as well. "The ABA," explains historian Tom Dyja, "helped to shift the balance of power in professional basketball to African-Americans by basing its existence on them and not pretending otherwise."[14]

"Basketball was originally invented as a white man's game," notes philosopher and diplomat Michael Novak, but in the post–World War II culture, its "mythos became more than urban. It became in a symbolic and ritual way uniquely black." Such was the result of the sport's sophistication, its flashy showmanship, and its association with urban cityscapes. "Basketball, although neither invented by blacks nor played only by blacks, came to allow the mythic world of the black experience to enter directly, with minimal change, into American life." Baseball was a game with black athletes, as was football, where at least the quarterback was going to be white. Basketball, by contrast, was a black game. Both baseball and football featured position differences and assumptions about intelligence that allowed fans to maintain their racial prejudices yet identify with teams featuring black players. But no professional sport was as associated with blackness as basketball.[15]

Basketball was associated with ethnicity almost from its inception. In the 1890s, "inner-city settlement houses became the breeding grounds for future interscholastic, collegiate, and professional stars," notes historian Steven Riess, "almost all drawn from inner-city ethnic groups." As teams began professionalizing in the 1920s, they grew from those ethnic enclaves. Jewish teams like the B'nai Brith All-Stars, Irish teams like the original Celtics, and African American teams like the Harlem Renaissance Five dominated.[16]

That urbanity, Riess notes, ultimately drew black players at or below the poverty line to basketball and consequently drove the perception of the game's blackness in the postwar period as it had its ethnicity prior to World War II. "Other young athletes may learn basketball," wrote historian Pete Axthelm in 1970, "but city kids live it." Basketball "is considered a city game in a society which romanticizes the pastoral," wrote Jeffrey Sammons a generation later. "It has no Ruth, Gehrig, Cobb, Dimaggio, or Mathewson, icons of a white athletic dominance of years gone by. Although basketball is probably far more American than baseball in its pace of play, constant action, and undeniably urban foundations, no enabling mythology has been created for or seen in it historically. Moreover, it is now a black game in numbers, superstars, culture, and symbols."[17]

John Matthew Smith notes that though the NBA had integrated by the mid-1950s, collegiate teams like UCLA, which had featured black stars since Ralph Bunche played guard for the Bruins in the 1920s, and the University of San Francisco, which featured stars like Bill Russell and K. C. Jones who would compete at the next level, had done so as well. Such successful collegiate teams normalized blackness as a part of organized basketball, further darkening the feeder system for the professional organization.[18] Russell's rise to professional prominence, along with that of Wilt Chamberlain, Oscar Robertson, Elgin Baylor, and Connie Hawkins, a group historian Nelson George calls "standard-bearers for the Black athletic aesthetic," normalized the black presence in professional basketball in the second half of the 1950s, "years marked by acceptance and infamy for Blacks." That being the case, the sport's move into the Deep South the following decade was racially significant.[19]

In many ways, race consumed New Orleans. The Ku Klux Klan in Louisiana experienced a resurgence after the Supreme Court's *Brown v. Board of Education* decision, and the White Citizens Council emerged as well. Louisiana's first and most prominent chapter of the Citizens Council was the Greater New Orleans chapter, founded in 1955 and led by Plaquemines Parish lawyer Leander Perez. Perez and the Greater New Orleans Citizens Council led protests and published pamphlets, newspapers, and articles arguing that integration would increase violent crime among the races. The organization contended that black Louisianans were illiterate, disease ridden, and generally inferior to white people. It would therefore be unfair and unsafe for Louisiana schools to integrate.[20]

In the wake of the Montgomery bus boycott, the NAACP began to pressure the New Orleans Public Service Company to end segregation on public busses and streetcars, arguing that legal precedent demanded it. In 1958 the company agreed, integrating public transportation in New Orleans. That same year, Louisiana governor Earl Long built a fully integrated branch of LSU in New Orleans. This school would eventually become the University of New Orleans. The White Citizens Council resisted the university's cre- ation, and state troopers were called to the premises just in case. But the new school began its first integrated semester peacefully.[21]

New Orleans's public school desegregation was more controversial. The case had been instigated by the NAACP's Legal Defense Fund and headed by Louisiana lawyer and civil rights activist Alexander Pierre Tureaud. Largely because of his effort, the US district court ordered the Orleans Parish School Board to come up with a desegregation plan. But the board stalled, leading to controversy that enveloped the population throughout much of 1960.[22]

In November 1960, two New Orleans public schools integrated. By the end of the week, white parents had pulled their children from the schools and enrolled them in private schools (or kept them out all together). On November 15, the Citizens Council held a massive rally. Leander Perez and others whipped the crowd into such a frenzy that a white mob began march- ing to the school board the next day. The police turned water hoses on the protesters, which deterred them but only made them angrier. Mob members then turned their attention to black bystanders, injuring almost twenty. After New Orleans mayor deLesseps Morrison tried to calm the white rebels by assuring them that the police department would not enforce the integra- tion order, an angry black population took to the streets, too. No one died during the protests, but more than one hundred casualties resulted. Almost all of the more than 250 people arrested were black. Two years later, the Archdiocese of New Orleans integrated the city's 153 Catholic elementary and high schools to much less violence and national fanfare.[23]

Thus by 1964, all of the city's primary and secondary schools had a mea- sure of desegregation. But New Orleans's resistance to such efforts took other forms. When the American Football League scheduled its All-Star Game for Tulane Stadium the following year, for example, angry white cit- izens banned the black players from bars and hotels. In response to their poor treatment, the athletes organized a boycott, refusing to play in the racist city. The AFL ultimately agreed with the players and moved the game to Houston. The incident not only showed New Orleans's racial scars, but also damaged Sunbelt boosters' efforts to bring professional sports to the city.[24]

Downey's ownership group for the New Orleans team included several local leaders and Sunbelt boosters, chief among them Charles Smither. Smither, unlike Downey, was a native, an insurance magnate who joined the state legislature from the city's Fourteenth District in the 1960s. The general agent for Union Central Life Insurance, Smither was a leader in the New Orleans Chamber of Commerce. He was also an old-line Mardi Gras krewe member and chair of the city's library board in the late 1950s. In the early 1960s, Smither advocated peaceful integration of New Orleans public schools, joining hundreds of prominent residents to write a "Declaration of Principles relative to Our Urgent School Problem" urging "compliance with the final decisions of the United States Supreme Court." His was the standard profile of a civic booster, a far cry from Downey and an even farther one from Jules Kimble. But in the early 1960s, Smither and his colleagues remained in the background—it was Downey's show.[25]

Columnist Peter Finney wished the team well, "although I would be less than honest if I didn't harbor some misgivings over this new venture." Those misgivings centered on market saturation, consumer demand, and the need for a solid television contract—all legitimate concerns for a new franchise in a new league. *States-Item* executive sports editor Art Burke was similarly skeptical. Pro basketball was "a marginal operation supported tenuously by a loyal core of fans who don't care whether it's a dunk or a double dribble—just so long as there's a round ball involved."[26]

In an attempt to bring the veneer of St. Louis and the NBA, Downey held a news conference in early February to announce his offer to Bob Pettit to be the team's coach and director of player personnel. Pettit had been a star player at LSU in the early 1950s. He had also led the St. Louis Hawks NBA championship team in 1958 and was thus the ideal connective tissue between St. Louis and Louisiana. Such was the reason for the press conference. "Bob said he would take the offer under advisement," Downey announced. "He is our first choice." It was a promoter's move. Pettit had simply been approached about the job and had committed to nothing, but the mention of his possible involvement gave the team its most substantial coverage to date.[27]

The veneer of the NBA, however, did not keep Downey from taking shots at the league that had excluded him. "We will have the best pension and insurance plan in any professional sport," he claimed in the Pettit press conference, referring to pension disputes between players and management in the NBA. The new league "will not disregard amateur basketball, [and] we will not fight with the Amateur Athletic Union or the National Collegiate Athletic Association," again referencing prominent NBA disputes. "We will have everything the National Basketball Association does not have," said Downey. That group "has no leadership and the commissioner is controlled by the owners of the clubs." Such would not be the case with the ABA.[28]

In announcing his interviews with NBA legends Dolph Schayes and Harry Gallatin for the New Orleans post, Downey made much the same attempt as he did with Pettit. He resorted to similar methods yet again in declaring that the team was courting star Dillard senior Marlbert Pradd. Downey offered Pradd $100,000 and encouraged him to give the ABA franchise the opportunity to match any offer from the rival NBA. In this early stage, explained the *Picayune*'s Ed Staton, "Downey's passion to field the team was ranked with missionary work among the headhunters, and defusing time bombs as a life's work."[29]

As time went on, however, Downey took a different tack, leaking information of possible signings then coyly refusing to confirm or deny them for reporters. The Canteen Corporation regional vice president had been in show business for years and had even grown up in it. He knew how to generate media. It was rumored that Downey had talked to the Boston Celtics' Bailey Howell, San Francisco's Clyde Lee, and New York's Willis Reed, a former All-American at Louisiana's Grambling State. More certain was the report that George Washington University coach Babe McCarthy, formerly of Mississippi State, had come to New Orleans to interview for the head coach and general manager position.[30]

James Harrison McCarthy was from Baldwyn, Mississippi. After coaching Mississippi State for ten seasons, winning four SEC championships, he had moved to coach George Washington University for one season before taking the New Orleans job. "Coaching jobs in professional basketball used to belong to fast-talking men from places like New York," wrote the *Picayune*'s Staton. "And you couldn't crack the lodge unless you could name the starting lineup of the Original Celtics. That is the way it used to be. That was before a lively group met and formed the American Basketball Association."[31] In the ABA, rural southerners could be pros.

McCarthy had brought his Mississippi State team to New Orleans often, both for its annual game with rival Tulane and its occasional games in the collegiate basketball tournament associated with the Sugar Bowl. But he was known in New Orleans for the same event for which he was known throughout the South—playing an NCAA tournament game against integrated Loyola University Chicago in 1963. When Mississippi State won that season's SEC championship, the team secured its third consecutive title and its fourth in five years. But McCarthy had never competed in the national tournament because of Mississippi's unwritten rule against playing integrated teams. He was determined to do so in 1963. "Now, since the James Meredith case at Ole Miss," he said, "they can't say, 'I told you so, you played against integrated teams and look what it brought on' because it didn't bring it on."[32]

And so, abetted by university president Dean Colvard, the team planned to play in the national tournament after defeating Tulane and clinching the SEC championship in New Orleans. The day before Mississippi State's players were scheduled to leave for East Lansing, Michigan, however, a state senator received a temporary injunction against the team's travel. McCarthy duped the sheriffs serving the injunction by flying out without his team. He sent the freshman squad to the airport in the varsity players' place, then secreted the latter out of town on a private plane the following day. Mississippi State lost its game with Loyola. Yet it helped tear down the edifice of segregated southern sports in the process.[33]

The league's first meeting was scheduled for early March in New Orleans. Downey used the publicity the event attracted to announce McCarthy's official hiring at a press conference at the Fontainebleau Hotel. McCarthy affected an air of humility while addressing the public, calling himself a "poor man's Red Auerbach." He was excited about the "great challenge" that "brings me close to home." By "home," he meant Mississippi, but argued, "I have always considered New Orleans my second home, having brought Mississippi State teams to play against Tulane University and four times had teams in the fine Sugar Bowl basketball tournament. It's good to be back."[34]

McCarthy was optimistic about the team's chances. "My hardest job will be to convince New Orleans that we are here," he said of his new job in the professional ranks. "If the city will join hands, we can make our team the best in the world. I know that in a city of one million people, there are thousands of fans who prefer basketball to other sports. We just have to let them know we are here."[35] The meeting was important for Downey in another way. After elections he found himself treasurer of the new league, joining president Gary Davidson, vice president Gabe Rubin, treasurer James Ackerman, and commissioner George Mikan to create a governing body. The group set a draft for later in March and created a seventy-game schedule. Downey himself announced, "We are presently studying three elaborate pension plans calling for in excess of the present demands of the NBA players."[36]

The next step for McCarthy, Downey, and the ABA was a collegiate draft, held in early April in Oakland. The Buccaneers made strategic picks, taking players from smaller colleges with ties to the region. With the second overall pick in the first round, the team took James Jones, a small All-American guard from Grambling. In the third round, Downey's group took Robert Allen, a forward from Arkansas AM&N in Pine Bluff. These black players from regional black colleges were prominent picks meant to compose the core of the young team. Though Dallas drafted Downey's coveted Marlbert Pradd, the Buccaneers gave up the next season's first-round pick and $20,000 to secure him as well. In later rounds, the Buccaneers took two players from Tulane and one from McNeese. The vast majority of the team's picks (twenty-one in that first draft) were from southern schools.[37]

The draft choices demonstrated that the team's leadership was more interested in pairing strong talent with a modicum of local interest than in playing to the racial politics of the late 1960s. Such would not be the case in Atlanta the following season. The other major southern city finally brought the NBA to the Deep South, closing a deal for the Hawks that Downey had been unable to secure. The Hawks' management responded to the racial climate of its city and potential fandom by dismantling a highly success-ful and largely black team and replacing it with a less successful but more marketable white one.[38] In New Orleans, however, locality and talent took precedence.

The *Louisiana Weekly*, New Orleans's black newspaper, followed Pradd's collegiate exploits closely. When Downey announced the city's new ABA franchise, the paper's principal interest was in the team's pursuit of Pradd and other players from the state's black colleges. "Downey stated that no contact had been made with Pradd," Jim Hall explained, "but he and a num-ber of college players from Grambling and Southern would be asked to join the Bucs." Pradd was a legitimate phenom in the city. When Downey made him an offer, the *Weekly* was celebratory in its reporting but noted that Pradd dreamed of playing in Chicago, his home city, at some point in his career. The paper was similarly jubilant about Grambling's James Jones. "If Marlbert Pradd and James Jones were to take up in the pro ranks where they left off in college," the *Weekly* predicted, "the New Orleans Buccaneers could take aim on the rest of the American Basketball Association with the deadliest double barrel scoring attack in the league." Sensing the enthu-siasm of black New Orleans based on the team's acquisition of local play-ers from black colleges, the Buccaneers took out large advertisements in the *Louisiana Weekly*. The notices promised "a new brand of pro basketball action!" and encouraged black fans to purchase tickets at Werlein's music store on Canal Street.[39]

Downey was keenly aware of the way race played in New Orleans. On the one hand, it lacked the standard pedigree of a Deep South city and was multicultural in a way that places like Atlanta were not. The year prior to the Buccaneers' inaugural season, for example, Steve Martin became the first black collegian to play in the Southeastern Conference when he started for the Tulane baseball team in his sophomore season. Two months prior to the announcement of the city's ABA franchise, the NFL granted New Orleans a football franchise that would obviously be integrated as well.[40]

At the same time, however, in May 1967, Downey and a group of four others, including Marlbert Pradd, entered Ched's Lounge on Canal Street.

When the manager said Pradd had to leave, Downey grew furious, screaming at the manager and denouncing the segregationist practice. He ran through the lounge to the bandstand and spoke to the bandleader. Tommy Dawn and The Sunsets were friends with Downey and knew of his reputation in the music business. "Tommy," said Downey, "stop playing. I'm with a black friend and they won't let us in the restaurant." And so the band stopped playing, packed their instruments, and left. "I know those guys," Downey told the manager. "They don't like playing in a restaurant where you won't let black people come in." Customers began leaving, too. The next month, the restaurant filed suit against Downey, claiming loss of business and reputation because of the incident. It took two years for the case to come to trial, but the jury ultimately ruled in Downey's favor.[41]

Three days prior to the Ched's incident, Pradd became the first player to sign with the new team. At a Buccaneer Day event staged by the Young Men's Business Club, Downey announced the signing of Pradd, of players from Tennessee and Mississippi, and of Doug Moe, a former Tarheel All-American who would become the team's best player in that first season. Downey also used the event to announce a deal with Loyola University New Orleans to play Buccaneer home games at Loyola Field House. In a speech to Loyola's Delta Sigma Pi business fraternity, he explained that the team would play a third of its games at the university and the rest at the downtown Municipal Auditorium. Downey also cited a survey that "indicated that professional sports could survive under the condition that there is a playing area and adequate parking," and he predicted that the team could survive on an average of only three thousand home spectators.[42]

Downey had approached Loyola about using the university's field house the day after acquiring the franchise in January 1967. He assured the dean of students, Joseph Malloy, that events would be scheduled around Loyola games and university events, but the school was wary of the prospect. Downey estimated four thousand ticket sales per game at $3.50 per seat, a figure Malloy rightly interpreted as "too optimistic." There was also the possibility that "professional sports on campus would tend to bring undesirable elements on campus." Mostly, however, Loyola officials believed that Downey was selling something he couldn't deliver. "Mr. Downey," Malloy concluded, "appears to be unduly optimistic about the future of professional basketball in New Orleans."[43]

By March, the university still doubted the efficacy of the project, school president Homer Jolley seeing its "many disadvantages." "Our immediate neighbors continually complain, both to us and the police, about inconveniences caused to them, such as cars being parked in their driveways, and about vandalism," worried Jolley. Professional games would only exacerbate such inconveniences. The intramural sports program and local concerts would pose further problems. "On the other hand," he noted, "since Loyola is apparently the only place in New Orleans where the professional team can play until other facilities are built, we do not want to offend the New Orleans community if a professional basketball team is important to the city." The university's lawyer agreed, conceding, "Apparently professional basketball, as also professional football, will be of importance to the City of New Orleans." As Tulane was making its football stadium available to the Saints, the attorney assumed that "Loyola would be criticized for refusing these facilities as I know Tulane would have been had they not made their stadium available to the Saints."[44]

Thus it was that Loyola agreed to provide access to Downey for Buccaneer home games, renting the facility for $1,000 per game against 12.5 percent gross. Malloy sent the team a list of potential open dates from which to choose for league games. "The University is making these dates available to you at considerable sacrifice of its own freedom of scheduling student events in the Fieldhouse," Malloy explained to Downey, "but we would like to make it possible for professional basketball to play in the City of New Orleans." Loyola, then, got a financial stake in home games and a sense of civic responsibility in the bargain. The Buccaneers, meanwhile, got the legitimacy that came from playing in the city's only respected basketball arena, home to collegiate Sugar Bowl tournaments and other games. The team also got the legitimacy of Loyola itself, a respected, long-standing, stable institution that could only benefit an upstart professional basketball league.[45]

In another press conference later that month, Downey announced the signing of Clyde Lee, a former Vanderbilt All-American who had played the previous season with the NBA's Western Division champion San Francisco

Warriors. "I wanted to get closer to home," said Lee, echoing the sentiment of his coach. Jumping to the upstart league would "give me the opportunity to play more and I honestly feel that the ABA and the New Orleans franchise have a lot on the ball. It's a challenge and I love New Orleans." Then the Buccaneers signed Bobby Love of the NBA's Cincinnati Royals. Another Louisiana native who had played at Southern University, Love was the "first Negro player ever to be named to the All-South team—an all-star team seldom frequented by small college players." Love, too, wanted to be closer to home.[46]

The *Times-Picayune*'s Nate Cohen could clearly see the Buccaneers' strategy. He noted that fans of the SEC and the Sugar Bowl basketball tournament would be familiar with the players from Vanderbilt and Tennessee, and he stated, "Love of Southern U., Dillard's Marlbert Pradd and Jim Jones of Grambling add local and statewide interest." Cohen asked McCarthy what he thought it would take for professional basketball to draw in New Orleans. "Any city or community no matter what size will either have or not have interest by the performance of the players," he said. "Tell me one city besides New York that turns out to laugh over a losing team like the Mets?" It was an optimistic philosophy, to say the least, but it would remain the cornerstone of McCarthy's and Downey's strategy.[47]

The team used a different strategy with Doug Moe. He was the Buccaneers' most talented player, but he wasn't local. He also had a past that included being banned from the NBA for a collegiate point-shaving scandal. Officials had discovered that Moe, while playing for the University of North Carolina, twice met with a gambler who tried to convince him to shave points. Moe argued that he had refused to cheat, but the gambler had given him seventy-five dollars in September and December 1960. Making the situation all the worse for Moe, he originally denied any involvement when interviewed by the school's chancellor, contradicting his court testimony. When that contradiction came to light, Moe was sent before the school's Honor Council, which absolved him of wrongdoing. Still, the chancellor then suspended him from campus indefinitely. The NBA would follow suit. The Buccaneers explained the scandal as a misunderstanding and reminded fans, "This guy is good enough to play with anybody. He's not only a fine ball player but a fine person, as well." Moe didn't drink, and he didn't smoke. South Carolina head coach Frank McGuire, who had been an assistant at North Carolina during Moe's time on campus, endorsed his former player, too: "If my son grows up with the same set of moral standards as Doug Moe, I'll consider my life a success."[48]

Downey was a showman and knew how to sell his players. As a disc jockey, he once rode a Ferris wheel nonstop for a week. Another time he bowled 150 straight games. Radio stations often promoted such stunts for charity, but Downey's experience with those events made the spectacle surrounding basketball promotion much easier. And it was spectacle with a clear goal in mind. "I'm almost certain that a 'war' will develop between the two leagues," said Downey, who also served as secretary of the ABA, "and it will end up like the battle between the National and American Football Leagues." I couldn't bring New Orleans an established NBA team, he seemed to be saying, but I can take the long route to get one. "Financially, the ABA couldn't be sounder. We started with more money than did the AFL."[49]

Things became more complicated for Downey and his team in early June, when the San Francisco Warriors filed a $1 million suit against Clyde Lee for jumping to the ABA's Buccaneers. Both Lee and Downey, however, put on a brave face. "I told San Francisco of the offer New Orleans had made, and they said, 'Oh, we could never match that,'" Lee explained. "I assumed there would be no counter offer, so I signed with New Orleans. And I have no regrets."[50]

The team had a similar problem trying to recruit the Cincinnati Royals' Bob "Butterbean" Love. A native of Bastrop, Louisiana, Love had played collegiately at Southern, and he returned to Baton Rouge to rehabilitate after a knee injury. Before the Royals began their NBA training camp in 1967, representatives from the Buccaneers made the short drive to Baton Rouge to attempt to convince Love to play in New Orleans. Star guard Rick Barry had moved from the NBA to the ABA in the Bay Area, and Connie Hawkins was with the Pittsburgh Pipers. With that kind of talent, Love thought the league might be viable. When New Orleans officials offered him a $16,000 contract, double his salary with the Royals, he signed. Cincinnati, however, was disinclined to allow the deal to happen. The NBA did not want to lose any more players, and the league and the Royals filed suit against New Orleans for tampering. They won, and Love would return to Cincinnati.[51]

Despite such setbacks, Downey's efforts on behalf of the city were paying off. Mayor Victor Schiro named him to the fire advisory board, for example. At the same time, however, Downey was in a period of transition. He ceded the team presidency to his colleague Charles Smither in early June, becoming the team's vice president and general manager instead. Soon after that, he passed the general manager's job to Babe McCarthy. Downey would remain the team's vice president, an alternate trustee to the league, and secretary of the ABA. But he needed to relieve himself of some of his duties "to pursue his other business obligations," namely his principal job with the Canteen Corporation. However, Downey's role didn't disappear. Just days after the announcement of Downey's reduced responsibilities, he attended league meetings in Pittsburgh and stumped to bring the ABA's inaugural All-Star Game to New Orleans.[52]

In July, the Canteen Corporation would call Downey away to New York. His friends and the team held a surprise farewell party for him at Kole's Corner in the French Quarter. Though he remained with the Buccaneers as vice president, Downey's imprint on the team—including its more problematic elements—was complete. For instance, the Buccaneers released Clyde Lee, probably fearing a lawsuit from the Warriors. Lee admitted that he had been in touch with his former team, but he had not agreed to return to San Francisco.[53]

The season started in October, but by November it was clear that Downey's work in New York would keep him from providing any significant help to the team. When he announced his resignation as vice president of the franchise, basketball's answer to Dave Dixon was gone.[54] Yet Downey's absence would not stop the pro basketball experiment from being unique. "The guy who really ran the team besides Babe McCarthy was Charlie Smither, who was the principal owner," remembered Larry Brown. "After games, I recall seeing Mr. Smither carrying the gate receipts out of the building in a shoe box." That the receipts would fit in a shoe box could not have been encouraging.[55]

Just prior to the preseason, the team signed former Grambling star John Comeaux, continuing to stoke black fans' interest. League play that first year merited full coverage in the *Louisiana Weekly*, which paid particularly close attention to the exploits of Pradd, Jones, and Comeaux.[56] The stars of the New Orleans team that first season, however, were Doug Moe and Larry Brown. Brown was serving as an assistant coach under Dean Smith when Babe McCarthy called him. Moe was playing in Italy. The two had been teammates at the University of North Carolina and were good friends. Thus Moe agreed to play if Brown played. To make his salary commensurate with Doug Moe's, Brown was also hired as the team's sports information director in the public relations department for the off-season. He was, according to the *Picayune*'s Howard Jacobs, "the 'midget' of the league," at a comparatively small five feet, ten inches tall.[57]

Brown and Moe "wondered if the league would get through a whole season. We figured if it did, it would be a miracle," said Moe. "We'd go to Minnesota and there would be more people on the floor than in the stands, then we'd go to Houston and it would be even worse than Minnesota. Anaheim, that was nothing but a joke. In New Orleans, we were okay. The only teams really doing any kind of job at the gate were Indiana and Kentucky."[58] New Orleans officials told players "to brown-bag it so they would have something to eat," explained Brown. "The team wasn't paying meal money and it sure wasn't going to supply food." Though the team carried twelve players, only ten traveled to road games to save money on airline flights. The trainer also stayed home, so the home team had to supply one. Prior to one game in Denver that first season, the trainer taped Brown's ankle so tight that it bled. He and his teammates cut off the tape. "So I went up to the trainer and asked him what he did in real life," said Brown. "I couldn't imagine that he did this for a living. The guy hesitated for a moment and said, 'Well, I'm a poultry farmer.'"[59]

Despite the team's and league's financial problems, the Buccaneers made it to the championship series in that first ABA season, facing the Pittsburgh Pipers. New Orleans took a 3-2 series lead with a Game 6 at home in the small Loyola gymnasium. The venue was unusually sold out for the championship, but the Bucs could not take advantage of home court. Pipers star Connie

Hawkins scored forty-one points, tying the series and making Pittsburgh's Game 7 victory almost a fait accompli. During that game, Pipers reserve Art Heyman punched a fan who spit on him. The fan, however, had a physical ailment and hadn't acted deliberately. So after the victory, New Orleans police entered the visiting locker room and arrested Heyman. The charges were dropped after Heyman realized his mistake and apologized.[60]

That final game in Pittsburgh's Civic Arena was delayed over an hour as a usually small crowd swelled to near capacity. The team averaged less than 1,500 fans at home games, but not for the final ABA contest. "We felt we were destined to win that game," said Pipers guard Charlie Williams. "We came out and just felt like we were going to win. We all knew we were going to win."[61]

The indignity of losing the series after being up three games to two with a home Game 6 was bad enough for the Buccaneers. But the situation worsened. Following the season, the team traded its two best players, Larry Brown and Doug Moe, to the Oakland Oaks for Steve Jones, who had been born in Alexandria. Despite Jones's roots, the trade was monumentally lopsided, removing two very good players and replacing them with one. In addition, the deal replaced two white stars with a black star. "After the trade, my career took off," Jones admitted. McCarthy moved the six-foot-five small forward to shooting guard, and the change was liberating for Jones. "I went from scoring 10 a game in Oakland to a shade under 20 in New Orleans, so leaving Oakland was fine with me."[62]

"When Oakland traded for me and Larry and only gave up Steve Jones," explained Doug Moe, "this had to be the most lopsided trade in the history of professional sports, bar none." And fitting the trade's lopsided nature, the Oaks, who had only won twenty-two games the previous season, won the title the next. New Orleans, meanwhile, never had that kind of success again. "I think New Orleans didn't think it had the money to pay Larry and me," said Moe. He had averaged 24 points and 10 rebounds in that first season in New Orleans and had placed second in votes for the league MVP title. Brown was considered one of the league's top point guards. Oakland's Bruce Hale orchestrated this curious deal, taking advantage of Moe's and Brown's desire for more money after their stellar opening season. The following season, the Buccaneers would lose to Moe's Oaks in the second round of the playoffs.[63]

But more substantial social problems were inherent in such deals as well. "My biggest concern was about being a black in New Orleans in 1968," remembered Jones. "There still were sit-ins, marches and other racial upheaval, which was not something I was used to." Jones described his inability to find a decent apartment, noting that he spent his first four months in New Orleans at the Sheraton on Canal Street. Buildings with clear vacancy signs claimed to be full when they saw that Jones was black. "I went apartment hunting every day, got rejected every day, and was unhappy every day." McCarthy suggested he live with Gerald Govan, a player in his second season with the team who had been living with a local black family, the common practice for black players. Even when the athletes made a group effort, they were frustrated. When Jones complained to the team's front office, the staff told him, "Well, you should have been here five years ago. Hey, five years ago they wouldn't even let you walk down Bourbon Street." That was the wrong answer. Jones demanded better housing or a trade. "I even went on television and said how I couldn't find a place to live," Jones explained. "There was a girl at one apartment complex who was fired for trying to help me. I finally found a place with the help of a black construction guy." It could be maddening. "Intellectually I understand what was going on, but that doesn't deny the fact that it hurt me and the other black players deeply."[64]

It demonstrated that a sympathetic leadership group and a racially progressive team did not translate to racial progressivism in New Orleans. Downey, Brown recalled, "used to go around town handing out these gold passes, which were lifetime passes to Bucs games. We'd have 350 people in the stands, and they all got in on those gold passes."[65] That lack of community interest in a predominantly black team in a predominantly black league would ultimately take its toll. Interest also waned because the Buccaneers were never able to match the success of that first season, as McCarthy had predicted. The team moved to Memphis in the league's fourth year, with McCarthy still the head coach.[66]

When the ABA held its second collegiate draft in May 1968, the *Weekly* again emphasized black locals, in particular Grambling's Richard Johnson and Southern's Jasper Wilson. Johnson was drafted in the second round, Wilson in the tenth. But their placement or potential to make the team was less important to black New Orleans than their relationship to Louisiana black colleges. The Buccaneers' big acquisition, however, was Steve "Snapper" Jones, and the *Weekly* emphasized the new arrival's potential to team with James Jones for another successful season.[67]

But the team wasn't particularly successful. While the Bucs made the playoffs again and demonstrated a slight increase in attendance, they failed to build on their good fortunes. Even the *Weekly* was losing interest, as its coverage of the team began to dissipate. For instance, when James Jones was named to the All-ABA team in 1969, the *Weekly* covered his selection with a wire story. By the time the New Orleans team moved to Memphis in the late summer of 1970, the sale merited one small column inch. For Jim Hall, "it was a sad day" when the move was announced, but "it would have been impossible for the Bucs to remain in New Orleans with the support given to them at the gate." Still, "for the average 2,000 paid patrons that supported the Bucs, they'll miss them."[68]

New team owner P. L. Blake, a friend of McCarthy's, authored the move to Memphis. But the team's downward spiral continued; it never had another winning season, and it had fewer fans than victories. The squad relocated to Memphis in the summer of 1970, so soon before the coming season that the city's Mid-South Coliseum didn't have enough open dates to accommodate a forty-two-game home schedule. So the Pros, as the Buccaneers were now called, played home games in Jackson, Tennessee, along with Memphis. The Pros also played in Greenville and Jackson, Mississippi. One of those Jackson, Mississippi, crowds had an announced attendance of only 465. Three months into its first season outside of New Orleans, Blake sold the team to Charlie Finley, claiming to have lost hundreds of thousands of dollars. The team would exist for two seasons as the Memphis Pros, two more as the Memphis Tams, and then one as the Memphis Sounds before moving to Baltimore in 1975. The Baltimore incarnation folded before it was ever able to play an ABA game.[69]

Low attendance had doomed the New Orleans Buccaneers, and the city and the media had moved on from the team by the time of its move north.

As the Buccaneers were leaving for Memphis, the *States-Item* reserved its excitement for former LSU guard Pete Maravich. He and his new pro team, the Atlanta Hawks, were coming to New Orleans to play a preseason game against the Philadelphia 76ers. "Mention the name Pete Maravich and people will talk all day about his exploits," the paper's Harry Martinez explained.[70]

As for Downey, he would not remain with Canteen Corporation long after moving to New York. His eclectic career would lead him to serve as an activist in Nigeria during the Biafran War in the late 1960s. After that, he started a consulting firm, Government Legislative Consultants, in Washington, DC, and spent several years in the 1970s as a lobbyist. Most notoriously, he began his controversial, conservative *Morton Downey Jr. Show* in 1987, wherein he paraded a series of bigotries before the country, becoming an infamous pariah in the process.[71] While Downey's talk show would only last two years, roughly the same amount of time he spent in New Orleans in the 1960s, it would make his name. Still, while the brash, outlandish caricature Downey evinced on his television program became the standard image of the polymath, in 1967 he was not only the father of professional basketball in New Orleans, but a racial pioneer who fought segregation and recruited players and coaches whose race and reputation flew in the face of the expectations of the city's whites.

Such refutes any previous mention of Downey's time with the Buccaneers. When acknowledged, Downey's participation with the team is noted as an oddity, as a piece of trivia. The otherwise infamous personality is described as having a brief, distanced financial stake in the ABA. These conclusions exist because Downey left the city so soon after the season began, but his participation was neither distanced, nor brief, nor trivial. He was a temporary civic booster whose actions flew in the face of southern racial mores and placed the cornerstone for professional basketball in New Orleans and the broader Deep South.

Ultimately, the city's disinterest in the Buccaneers would take the team to Memphis, but its three-year stint in New Orleans was longer than those in many ABA cities. In 1974, the continued boosterism led to an expansion franchise in the NBA, the New Orleans Jazz, which would stay in Louisiana until 1979. However, the development of professional basketball in New Orleans, and the racial assumptions that accompanied it, would not have been possible without the dogged effort and racial egalitarianism of a temporary transplant known more than anything else for his loudmouthed bigotry. It was, to be sure, a paradox. But in a city of paradox, that may have fit New Orleans even more than professional basketball.

3

WHEN HAWKS FLY SOUTH

Among the players trickling into Atlanta following the arrival of the first NBA team in the Deep South was "Pogo" Joe Caldwell, one of the stars of the former St. Louis Hawks. While in Missouri, the team was champion of the league's Western Division, 1968 regular season champion, and a perennial power. Caldwell was an all-star, a former standout at Arizona State, and a member of the gold medal–winning 1964 US Olympic team. He and his wife, daughters, and sister arrived at the Holiday Inn in Atlanta, only to be greeted by a carful of whites who screamed, "Hey, niggers!" before driving away. "Well," Caldwell's sister told him, "you're in the South now, brother."[1]

Professional sports had already arrived in Atlanta and the Deep South when the Hawks began playing at Georgia Tech's Alexander Memorial Coliseum. The move of the Milwaukee Braves, the impact of their black star Hank Aaron, and the country's poetic, fraught historical relationship with baseball and its role in race relations are generally interpreted as paving the way for first the NFL and then the NBA. This interpretation is instructive and, in a broad sense, true. What it ignores, again, is that neither of those sports was directly associated with blackness as was basketball. Even though the move was largely spurred by Sunbelt business imperatives that drove similar changes across the landscape of professional sports, race would matter greatly once the team arrived in Atlanta. Selling a black team and a black league to a white South in the 1960s was a significant chore. The city acquired the Hawks less than a month after the assassination of Martin Luther King Jr. Before the team's first game in Atlanta, Tommie Smith and John Carlos would bring the threat of Black Power into every white southern home.

Management responded by dismantling a highly successful and largely black team and replacing it with a less successful but more marketable white one. In this case, the economics of the South actually worked against the economics of the Sunbelt. A business designed to be a lucrative metropolitan status symbol for the "city too busy to hate" eroded under the racial weight placed upon it by the citizens who made that status symbol possible. Georgia wasn't hostile to the Hawks in any sustained way. But its lethargy was unequivocally racial and carried racial consequences that bled beyond the bounds of sports.

When Boston Braves owner Lou Perini realized in the early 1950s that even with a winning team, he couldn't compete locally with the Red Sox, he decided to move his franchise to Milwaukee, where he owned a Braves minor-league farm team. Fans flocked to the ballpark when the team won the World Series in 1957, but attendance faltered after the championship— and after the novelty of professional baseball wore off. In 1962 Perini sold the team to a group of investors hoping to relocate to Atlanta. These backers capitalized on the lack of any other baseball team within seven states, and they did so through the one medium that would explode professional sports in the Sunbelt: television. The Braves' first television contract in Atlanta was worth $2.5 million.[2]

After the Braves came the NFL's Falcons. Atlanta mayor Ivan Allen Jr. sought sports teams to validate the city's growing success, burnishing Atlanta's reputation as a "major-league" place. He once bragged that the city built Fulton County Stadium, the Braves' and Falcons' original home, "on ground we didn't own with money we didn't have for clubs we had not yet signed." But while the stadium was important—the principal cog in discussions of Sunbelt business imperatives and metropolitan infrastructure growth—television was more so. It made sports more accessible, and it turned them into soap operas. Ballplayers weren't faraway, seeming shrunken when viewed from a distant seat. They were closeup. They were replayed. They had life stories. Sports became personal.[3]

Tom Cousins, however, concerned himself less with television than with more traditional notions of infrastructure, principally the revitalization of downtown Atlanta. A sports coliseum would be the center of this renewal. "I was concerned with developing sixty acres of downtown Atlanta," he explained. "A coliseum was the key to the whole thing, some focal point to build around." Cousins was a prominent real estate developer whose land in downtown Atlanta would be worth much more if the area could be populated with businesses that catered to the now-suburban middle class. Such was a rarity for Sunbelt reclamation projects, which typically allowed businesses to follow the migrations of their citizens, thus creating their telltale sprawl.[4] Cousins's boosterism and financial interest in the downtown area situated his involvement in professional basketball and reversed the development trends of the 1960s. He sought to increase the value of his city property, which was losing value because of white Atlanta residents' out-migration to the suburbs. That migration was part of what historian Kevin Kruse terms white Atlanta's "fluid relationship" with the changing state of segregation in the face of the gains of the civil rights movement. The suburban exodus eliminated potentially ugly racial confrontations and allowed white Atlanta to congratulate itself on its relative progressivism.[5]

Downtown gentrification would do much the same thing. It priced poor black residents out of the construction area while keeping suburban white Atlantans engaged with the city center, preserving those white economies' ties to downtown and perpetuating the pleasing myth of racial accord. Postwar stadium construction "erased" much of the "urban diversity" of downtown neighborhoods, explains Benjamin Lisle. "Postwar modern stadiums relocated sports space from old urban neighborhoods to open sites along freeways, convenient to booming white suburbs or as anchors to clean-sweep downtown redevelopment." They were "idealized as playgrounds for the affluent" and thus "integrated new consumer spaces" into the construction.[6]

One such stadium was Houston's Astrodome, in many ways a precursor and impetus for the Superdome. Despite rapid metropolitan growth in the 1950s, as historians Robert C. Trumpbour and Kenneth Womack explain, "almost no one looked at Houston as a 'Major League' city with a high-culture reputation." The Astrodome was the city's attempt to change that perception by wooing professional sports to the city. To help facilitate the project, city leaders got the support of black businessman Quentin Mease, who, along with other black leaders, agreed to champion the project on the condition that it would be fully integrated.[7]

Cousins had the same goal for Atlanta and originally planned to build an arena to woo a professional team, but Ivan Allen warned him off. He explained that he went that route before securing the NFL's Falcons for the city, and that his efforts had almost backfired. "Get your franchise first," Allen told Cousins. "Then we'll build a coliseum." So the developer simply followed Allen's advice. "That's the reason I bought the Hawks," said Cousins. "I needed them to get the development going." To that end, he teamed with attorney and former governor Carl Sanders and purchased a basketball team for Atlanta.[8]

Ben Kerner and Leo Ferris founded the team as the Buffalo Bisons in 1946, the same year the Boston Celtics and New York Knickerbockers joined the Basketball Association of America, forerunner of the NBA. The Southern Basketball League had been created the year before. Among other players, the Bisons included William "Pop" Gates, former star of the Harlem-based Renaissance Big Five barnstorming team of the 1930s and 1940s. Gates, who had played his college basketball at Atlanta University, integrated the Bisons and the league the year prior to Jackie Robinson's 1947 Dodgers debut. Thus the team that became the Hawks began the original blackening of the NBA.[9]

From Buffalo, Kerner moved the team to the Mississippi River, locating in the area of Rock Island, Illinois; Moline, Illinois; and Davenport, Iowa. He also renamed the team the Tri-Cities Blackhawks after the area's infamous Black Hawk War. The new locale had a small-town mentality, and no hotel in Moline would house Gates. Kerner wouldn't invite him back for the 1947–48 season.[10] Then it was on to Milwaukee (a larger market that Kerner hoped could provide more profit) where the newly named Hawks suffered through a span of losing seasons. Those losses ensured that profit wouldn't come, and in 1955 the team moved again, this time to St. Louis. Under the leadership of general manager Marty Blake and the play of star Bob Pettit, the team began to have real success. It made the NBA finals in its second St. Louis season, losing a seven-game series to the Celtics in 1957. The following year, the Hawks improved again, winning the franchise's only championship after a six-game series with the Celtics. The Hawks would be the last all-white championship team in the NBA.[11]

Bill Russell was the star of those Celtics teams and one of the individuals principally responsible for both stabilizing the NBA and beginning the process of its blackening. When Russell debuted, only fifteen black players competed in the NBA. He would be the first iconic national black figure in the league, taking his place among the likes of Jesse Owens in track, Joe Louis in boxing, and Jackie Robinson in baseball. Russell became a representation of the race in his chosen sport, and he did so two years after *Brown v. Board of Education*. When Wilt Chamberlain entered the league in 1959, his rivalry with Russell drove the success of the NBA through the next decade. "Never before have so many people taken an active interest in professional basketball," wrote *Sport* magazine's Barry Gottehrer. "Suddenly, housewives and college coeds who generally avoid athletic events with a passion are taking sides in this battle between the giants."[12]

But not in the South. The Chamberlain-Russell rivalry dominated coverage of professional basketball and thus contributed to whites' assumption that the NBA was a black league, fundamentally different from the segregated high school and college contests in the region. In February 1966, *Sport* magazine's controversial article wondered aloud whether the NBA was developing too many black athletes for its own good. One former player told a reporter that he couldn't bear to watch the 1965 All-Star Game because seven of the ten starters were black. "I was disgusted," he said. "There were just too many of them. I couldn't get interested in watching them play."[13]

Meanwhile, Russell used his success to participate in the civil rights movement, leading marches in Boston and participating in others like the March on Washington. He also took part in Freedom Summer in Mississippi in the summer of 1964. "I don't like most white people because they are white," Russell famously announced in the early 1960s. "Conversely, I like most Negroes because they are black. Show me the lowest, most downtrodden Negro and I will say to you that man is my brother." By 1965, almost half of the NBA's players were black. Television ratings were up, as was the NBA's overall popularity. But the league's blackness, combined with statements like Russell's, only stoked southern white sports fans' racial skepticism about the viability about the NBA in their region.[14]

Russell's least favorite place to play was St. Louis, which many in the 1950s and early 1960s considered the most racist NBA city. Before the Celtics and Lakers became championship rivals, the Hawks dominated the Western Division and provided an annual challenge for the Celtics. The two played for the NBA championship in 1957, 1958, 1960, and 1961. In December 1956, the Celtics played a game in St. Louis's Kiel Auditorium. "The ball went up and Bob Pettit of the Hawks and I jumped for it," recalled Russell.

"'Coon.

"'Go back to Africa, you baboon.

"'Watch out, Pettit, you'll get covered with chocolate.

"'Black nigger.

"There was no doubt who the fans were yelling at," Russell said. "I was the only Negro athlete on either team."[15] This kind of reaction didn't encourage management to invest in black players, but ultimately the Hawks would have no choice. St. Louis was still an ostensibly southern town with pervasive segregationist policies. The fan base was white and had racialized expectations of its team. Lenny Wilkens was the second black player in St. Louis history, arriving in 1960 to join Sihugo Green, who had signed the year prior. Black players were expected to rebound the ball and pass to the white stars. This racial mixing was new, and most white players, like LSU's Bob Pettit, Kentucky's Cliff Hagan, and Kansas's Clyde Lovellette, had never played with black athletes.[16]

When Green, for example, turned over the ball, as David Halberstam noted, "the whites would not say anything, they would simply raise their eyebrows as if to say, *what can you expect, that's the way they are*." Away from the court, things weren't much better. Wilkens once received twenty-five dollars for a promotional event in St. Louis, while his white teammates Bob Pettit and Cliff Hagan received seventy-five dollars. "That was St. Louis," wrote Halberstam.[17]

St. Louis was also particularly difficult for visiting black players. It could be "the loneliest town in the world." Bill Russell had experienced brief racial attacks in college, "but in St. Louis it was 'baboon . . . nigger . . . black bastard.' Not from the players. Never have I heard a professional ballplayer say anything about race in a game. But the fans were using it as a weapon." Russell called the city "the St. Louis of my bitter memories," and it was notorious throughout the league.[18]

Still, times were changing. In 1962, the Hawks drafted Zelmo Beaty, Bill Bridges, and John Barnhill, three more black players who would be quality contributors. In 1964, general manager Marty Blake drafted Paul Silas from Creighton, and the following year he acquired Joe Caldwell in a trade with Detroit. In 1966, he drafted Lou Hudson from Minnesota. Meanwhile, after the 1965 season, injuries forced the retirement of Pettit, the team's one legitimate superstar.[19] In the span of the early sixties, black players came to dominate the team (and much of the league).

There was, however a danger in such growth. "As the game became more exciting, faster, blacker," explains Halberstam, "it was moving ahead of the fans' capacity to accept it." During the 1967–68 season, the new crop of talent led the team to again win the Western Conference regular season title (though the Hawks would be upset in the first round of the playoffs). That team won fifty-six games and lost twenty-six— a franchise record. And yet the Hawks had drawn just over five thousand fans to its home games in Kiel Auditorium, which had a capacity of nine thousand. The venture was still profitable, but there was clearly more to be had. Kerner had also tried and failed to persuade the city to build a new arena. And so the team's founder decided to sell.[20]

When the American Basketball Association arrived to challenge the hegemony of the NBA, it sought to put teams in new, emerging markets so they could be successful without directly competing with the established league. Teams like Downey's New Orleans Buccaneers demonstrated that, despite the South's history, the region could be a viable professional basketball market.[21] Though crowds were small in southern venues, the league itself proved resilient. The ABA forced the NBA to simultaneously consider expanding to stem the tide of the new league and possibly moving into a southern market. Moreover, the association put Kerner, whom Halberstam calls "one of the last of the old-style owners," at a decided disadvantage. The growth of the ABA made acquiring a cheap franchise relatively easy; by extension, it made selling an established NBA team that much more difficult. Kerner had been public about his wish to sell the Hawks the previous season, announcing in early January 1967 that he hoped to sell the squad to "either local interests or other cities." He negotiated first with Downey's investment group from New Orleans, but the deal collapsed when Kerner found it unacceptable. That bungled sale to a would-be Louisiana owner generated negative publicity, and so negotiations in 1968 would continue privately.[22]

"Without the backstage maneuvering, the private eye implications, and the CIA intrigue, it might never have been possible for Georgia's capital city to obtain its fourth professional franchise," the *Atlanta Daily World*'s Marion Jackson explained. That lack of publicity led to surprise in Atlanta when, on Friday, May 3, Tom Cousins and Ben Kerner announced that the NBA was officially coming to the Deep South. The news broke less than a month after the assassination of Martin Luther King, while the wounds that murder caused were still gaping.[23]

It was an unlikely convergence of time and place. Following King's assassination on April 4, riots erupted in Washington, DC, Chicago, Baltimore, Kansas City, and more than one hundred other urban areas nationwide. The uprisings demonstrated to many across the country that black radicalism was not limited to Harlem, Oakland, and Watts. They scared and confused many whites who had trouble reconciling urban violence with the death of a nonviolent leader.[24] That radicalism also permeated sports. As the King riots raged, sociologist Harry Edwards was leading the Olympic Project for Human Rights and organizing a boycott of the 1968 Summer Olympics in Mexico City to protest race inequality and the marginalization of the black athlete.[25] On April 28, well within the depths of the King and Olympic maelstroms, Muhammad Ali celebrated the one-year anniversary of his refusal to report after the United States Army drafted him to fight in Vietnam. Ali's defiance led boxing officials to strip him of the heavyweight championship and ban him from the sport.[26]

Meanwhile, Atlanta was struggling with its own long history of race conflict. In the Gilded Age, black schools and churches created concentrations of black citizens that became segregated enclaves prior to the turn of the century. Such areas could be a help or a hindrance. In the 1920s, for example, Atlanta elected a Ku Klux Klan mayor and served as headquarters for the newly revived organization. In 1952, however, Rufus Clement, president of Atlanta University, was able to take advantage of that segregated voting bloc to win a seat on the Atlanta school board. He became the city's first elected black official since the nineteenth century.[27]

Clement's ability to win and Atlanta public officials' lack of overt grandstanding racism in the 1950s and 1960s were the result of a large black voting base that could prevent virulent racists from winning. That was good, but it provided Atlanta with an undeserved reputation for racial moderation that ignored the problems of employment discrimination, pay disparity, segregation, unequal city services, and inadequate education. As historian Maurice J. Hobson has demonstrated, Atlanta's middle- and upper-class population played a vital role in the city's rise to prominence. Yet at the same time, those black residents in the lower class were some of the most impoverished in the nation. And as the Sunbelt success of Atlanta continued to grow, "Atlanta's black working class became increasingly disenfranchised as the larger city was franchised within a global economy," despite the fact that black participation helped create that growth.[28]

The city's reputation for racial progressivism masked this reality, but activists knew better. On May 5, two days after the announcement about the Hawks, Ralph Abernathy led a group on the "Southern leg" of the Poor People's March on Washington, heading to Atlanta from Alabama. They would arrive on May 8.[29] Thus the Hawks appeared in Atlanta at the intersection of national racial tumult and local metropolitan political realities. "Professional Basketball Hits Atlanta Like A Sledgehammer," the *Daily World*'s sports editor, Marion Jackson, announced. His only initial public worry, however, was not about race or politics. Instead, Jackson feared the team's arrival brought with it the potential for oversaturation, as the city had been acquiring professional teams in all of the major sports. "IS ATLANTA STRETCHING TOO FAR in major league sports?" he asked.[30]

The confluence of race and location pressed upon not only the decision to bring the team to Georgia, but also the venue in which it would play. Kerner, in fact, originally hesitated to sell to Cousins and Sanders because he assumed that the NBA would never approve a deal that did not include an arena. Cousins therefore signed a contract with Georgia Tech to use Alexander Memorial Coliseum. The arrangement was good enough for Kerner, though the stadium barely met league standards, if at all. "The Tech people were great to us and very gracious," said Marty Blake. "But it was a bad building. It had terrible locker rooms and only seated about 7,200. The league wouldn't have approved it, but Benny Kerner was one of the pioneers of pro basketball, and the league people wanted to see him get out of the business with some money."[31]

Tech was an interesting choice. Later in 1968, the university would hire its first black instructor, William Peace, in the Department of Social Sciences. Students would also found the school's first black student organization, the Georgia Tech African American Association. In 1969, Tech welcomed Eddie McAshan, its first black scholarship football player. It wasn't until 1971 that Karl Binns integrated Georgia Tech's basketball team, which typically played in Alexander Memorial.[32]

The league, however, was less concerned with the temporary building and more concerned with the construction of a permanent arena, and assurances from the Atlanta ownership group that one would be ready in two years cemented the deal. Cousins shared the NBA's concern. The Hawks' new owner had commissioned a study as to the best way to develop downtown Atlanta and capitalize on his land rights in the city. The review argued that an arena was the lynchpin of urban development, so he purchased the Hawks. But Cousins wasn't necessarily interested in basketball. "In the four years I went to the University of Georgia, I probably went to one game," he remembered. "The last basketball game I played was with an Atlanta Athletic Club team," said Cousins. "I was matched against Ewell Pope and he broke two of my ribs." Nevertheless, the game still mattered for the players, and Tech's old, poorly lit coliseum featured a floor placed directly over hard, unforgiving concrete.[33]

Cousins, according to the *Atlanta Journal*'s Jim Minter, would "be in position to be the prime mover if not the builder of a new Madison Square Garden type arena in Atlanta." Cousins certainly understood the responsibility, stating, "We wouldn't have been able to buy the Hawks on the strength of playing in the Tech Coliseum." Despite the relative inadequacy of Tech's arena, its use was a subtle coup. "In the past," Minter reported, "the school has stoutly resisted any move by professional teams to play on the campus." That resistance seemed certain for basketball, with the added impetus of race thrown into the bargain. But two factors changed that dynamic. First, Alexander Memorial was on the edge of campus and thus wouldn't affect school activities (Tech used this claim to deny the Falcons the opportunity to play exhibitions at Grant Field, which was in the middle of campus). Second, the school, not the athletic department, owned the coliseum, and the school had proven far more progressive than the sum of its sports programs.[34]

"When the St. Louis Hawks swooped down upon us this weekend from the blue, we were not prepared," admitted an editorialist for the *Journal*. "All of a sudden, we had the St. Louis Hawks. Rather, the Atlanta Hawks. Tomorrow we expect to read that someone has brought us Madison Square Garden. That is, Margaret Mitchell Square Garden. For a moment, we felt like a wife whose husband has brought her home 300 pounds of bass, and no deep-freeze." Based on a study by the Atlanta-Fulton Recreation (Stadium) Authority, Cousins was targeting the area around Spring Street and the Techwood viaduct. If situated near the football stadium and with its parking projects already under way, the cost of the entire endeavor could come in at around $19 million. The board of aldermen, however, commissioned a study "for the placement and erection of a coliseum with a seating capacity of 15,000 within the Civic Center complex," though the Spring Street–Techwood viaduct area was still an option. The studies had a common emphasis on the gentrification of downtown Atlanta. If nothing else, "Margaret Mitchell Square Garden" would help whiten the area around it.[35]

Sanders was optimistic about the prospect. The lawyer and onetime governor from Augusta had been a backup quarterback for the University of

Georgia and a reserve player on the school's basketball team, but he was a political animal more than anything else. He argued just days after the announcement of the Hawks' move that a new basketball arena in downtown Atlanta could draw the 1972 Democratic National Convention. The Hawks meant a new coliseum, "and if the coliseum is in operation by 1972, then Atlanta certainly could be considered for the party convention," Sanders argued. It would be "one of the greatest things that could happen to the South. It would really put us in the mainstream of America."[36]

The NBA was just as interested in the urban revitalization project. Commissioner Walter Kennedy clearly wanted to approve the transfer—mostly to help Kerner, who had been so vital to the early development of the league—but still made the deal contingent on Atlanta's ability to build a new arena. The Hawks had their introductory press conference at the downtown Marriott on May 16, and Carl Sanders attended, along with Kennedy. Hawks forward Bill Bridges claimed to welcome the change, hoping for more fan interest. "We filled up the building one time [in St. Louis]," said Bridges, "and that was for a doubleheader with the Globetrotters. The crowd came to see the Globetrotters."[37]

Bridges certainly had a point. The Hawks' playoff attendance in 1968 was poor. Against the San Francisco Warriors, Kiel crowds numbered just over five thousand for two games, and when the third St. Louis game moved to Washington University because of a prior commitment, attendance fell to around four thousand. Kerner cited that disappointment as affecting his decision to sell. Still, Bridges may have been searching for a diamond in a sea of coal. "I was surprised but not really shocked," said center Zelmo Beaty about the sale. "I haven't talked with the owners yet and haven't collected my ideas about it. I always felt Atlanta was a possibility. Atlanta has a complete sports field."[38]

Bridges and Beaty were stars, but Bridges and Beaty were black. Despite poor St. Louis attendance figures—and poor treatment of black athletes in the city—an assumption that Deep South racial beliefs would make things worse for black players prevailed. Beaty and Bridges, Joe Caldwell and Jim Davis, Lou Hudson and Paul Silas, and Lenny Wilkens, the team's biggest star, were all black. The Hawks were a good team. They were the defending

Western Division champions in 1968. But they were black, and they were coming to a Deep South Sunbelt city that was gentrifying part of its downtown to make room for them. They were playing initially at an arena whose usual team, Georgia Tech's Yellow Jackets, had yet to integrate.[39] Regardless of the Sunbelt business imperatives that drove stadium construction in Atlanta, the organization would always have to deal with race.

In an effort to broaden interest in the team beyond the Atlanta city limits, the Hawks hired a local public relations director, Richard Hyatt, an assistant sports information director at Georgia Tech. Among his other duties, Hyatt toured the state, speaking at civic clubs, calling on the media, and trying to sell the NBA to citizens of Macon, Rome, Columbus, and other cities. The people to whom he spoke knew Bill Russell. They knew Wilt Chamberlain. But they did not know much more than that, and race was always a concern. At a civic club speech in Macon, someone in the audience asked, "Are there any white players in this league?" Hyatt told him about the Hawks' Gene Tormohlen and Don Ohl. "What about the league itself?" was the response. "Aren't the main ones all black?" Similar questions happened at every public relations stop. Even more problematic for Hyatt, those questions didn't just come from fans. Sportswriters in smaller Georgia cities were asking the same questions.[40]

When the Hawks went on the road to play an exhibition game against Chicago in Auburn, Alabama, the black players struggled to get service at a local restaurant. After finally getting food after repeated demands, Caldwell claimed that they left the waitress "a penny tip to remind her that Abe Lincoln freed the slaves almost a century ago and that we are all equal human beings." Still, to be fair, Atlanta was not tiny Auburn, Alabama. "While conditions weren't up to par," said Caldwell, "the people of Atlanta were first-class." Besides, the problems for players were far more nuanced than that.[41]

Lenny Wilkens was runner-up to Wilt Chamberlain in the 1968 MVP vote, but he made $30,000 per year in comparison to Chamberlain's $250,000. Kerner was known as the cheapest owner in the NBA. As David Halberstam notes, "One year he boasted to Wilkens that he had run the entire club for $100,000." Wilkens wanted a modest $60,000 per year in response to his runner-up season and the discrepancy between his earnings and Chamberlain's, yet the team only offered him $40,000. Atlanta fully expected to have Wilkens, as Atlanta newspapers featured him prominently in articles about the incoming team. "I really don't think Lennie will be any problem," said Blake, "and to be honest, we're not too worried about him. He'll play, I'm sure of that." But Wilkens held out. The team responded by fining him for not reporting to camp, then trading him to Seattle for Walt Hazzard. The last thing the new black team in the Deep South needed was a militant, uppity black man making rights claims to white southerners. "They're going to love Walt Hazzard in Atlanta," wrote the *Journal's* Teague Jackson. Even Ben Kerner weighed in, absurdly arguing, "Hazzard is a better ballplayer, he has quicker hands than Lennie." Such was the variance in the racism of city and town. Wilkens could easily have eaten in almost any Atlanta restaurant, but he couldn't get fair pay for his value.[42]

In any event, the most significant problems existed for the players who weren't traded. "By 1968, when Wilkens finally left, the Hawks—now in Atlanta—were on their way to becoming one of the first great black basketball teams in the league," Halberstam explains. "The old white stars had gradually moved on, to be replaced by talented blacks like Wilkens, Zelmo Beaty, Bill Bridges, Paul Silas, Joe Caldwell, Lou Hudson, all exceptional players and role players as well." But the team was keenly aware of the role race played in the region. It responded to its move to the Deep South by drafting South Carolina's Skip Harlicka, Vanderbilt's Bob Warren, and Miami's Rusty Parker, three white players from southern schools who would never live up to whatever marginal hype they received. The Hawks clearly made these moves with at least some recognition of their new fan base. Or, in the words of Halberstam, "For a time, five blacks started; then a white player was obtained so that at least one white could start at home, and Joe Caldwell, averaging nearly twenty points a game, went, much to his displeasure, to the bench."[43]

Bob Warren was white and southern, but he wasn't quite good enough to make the team. The Hawks encouraged him to sign with the ABA in July. Skip Harlicka wouldn't make the squad, either, joining the army instead. The Hawks also acquired rookie Dick Nemelka. The former Brigham Young star had been serving his Mormon mission in Australia for two years and was finally ready to join the Hawks, who had drafted him in 1966. In June, the team signed white forward Ron Krick from the University of Cincinnati. In late August, the Hawks signed Jim Davis, who had played with the team before, prior to a two-year stint in the Eastern League. Davis replaced Gene Tormohlen, who retired as a player to become one of coach Richie Guerin's assistant coaches. Jim Davis was the team's only black acquisition. Through the draft and other roster maneuvers, the whitening of the Hawks had begun. However, its early success in the task was marginal because the acquired players weren't good enough to make the team. Don Ohl was the only white player listed as a member of the Hawks in the *Atlanta Journal's* introduction of the players to the city in early May, and he and Arizona State's Dennis Hamilton would be the only white players on the team on opening day.[44]

That left the black players wondering about their place on the team and in the town. Richard Hyatt picked up Joe Caldwell from the Atlanta airport on one of his early visits to the city. Once Hyatt drove Caldwell and his wife to the downtown Mariott, Caldwell looked at him and observed, "I haven't seen anybody in a white hood yet." Caldwell and his fellow players came to Atlanta armed with stereotyped expectations of the South and their own personal worries about racial interactions. Combined with the legitimate, if more subtle, white racism that did exist in the city and the region, those kinds of reactions created a combustible situation for everyone involved.[45]

The team then embarked on a chaotic first season in Atlanta. Starting slowly while adjusting to the loss of Wilkens, the Hawks' record was 12-15 after a loss to the Lakers on December 6. But the group recovered. A subsequent twelve-game winning streak in December and January led to larger crowds.[46] The floor at Tech also continued to be a problem during the season. It was so hard that Guerin ordered the team to change practice venues in early November, and the athletes held workouts at the city's Jewish community center. The team also stayed in the news with strange incidents, like the time in January when Richie Guerin assaulted a Philadelphia sportswriter. The Hawks finished their first Atlanta season 48-34, placing second in the Western Division behind the Lakers. Ultimately, the team lost the division finals to the Lakers four games to one. (As Atlanta lost Lenny

Wilkens in a trade with Seattle, Los Angeles gained Wilt Chamberlain in a trade with Philadelphia.)[47]

Though the team was obviously competitive, attendance wasn't strong in that first season. Management responded by further whitening the Hawks at the expense of their talent. That off-season, Zelmo Beaty left the team for the ABA, and Guerin traded all-star Paul Silas for white forward Gary Gregor. "That was the worst deal I made as a coach," Guerin said later. "Gregor had played well in his first two years, and I wanted him as another big scoring forward. But the trading of Paul Silas was another part of the team's demise." It was certainly part of the team's demise, but Guerin's claim that he really wanted Gregor is questionable at best. Not only had Gregor only played one NBA season (not two) when the trade happened, his statistics were not significantly better than Silas's. He was another southern white player from the University of South Carolina. Again, race was either a conscious or subconscious motivation.[48]

The draft also belied racial thinking. In April 1969, the Hawks took star Louisville guard Butch Beard in the first round and Wally Anderzunas of Creighton in the second. While Beard was black, none of the team's other picks were. Team officials took Billy Hahn from Tennessee in the fourth round, Guy Mackner of South Dakota in the sixth, and Bob Bundy of Vanderbilt in the seventh. With the new crop of white players filling out the roster, Atlanta seemed more excited about its professional basketball team. WSB-TV had broadcast the team's first Atlanta game in its first season, but the station increased its commitment in the second season to eight games. WSB radio would broadcast every Hawks game.[49]

Of course, media interest wasn't entirely related to the changing racial makeup of the team. The Hawks' first Atlanta season was successful, and television and radio stations assumed (erroneously, in this case) that victories would drive fan interest. The problem with such assumptions, however, was that popularity stemming from the prospect of seeing white players did not necessarily translate into success on the court. The Hawks began the 1969–70 season strongly, going 12-3 in the team's first fifteen games. But the poor personnel moves ultimately took their toll. On February 1, the Hawks were 32-26 with a four-game losing streak. Blake responded by acquiring

Walt Bellamy from Detroit. Bellamy filled holes in the team's rebounding and led Atlanta to a 15-6 finish; his play (along with Laker injuries) helped the Hawks win the regular-season Western Division crown. In the conference finals, however, the healthy Lakers dominated the Hawks four games to none. A successful franchise was eroding, calcifying at the hands of racial politics. And that erosion hurt the season's early popularity. Attendance during the 1969–70 season was less than 5,000 per game. That lackluster showing resulted in part from Atlanta's identity as a southern town concerned almost solely with college football. But race also mattered. The team had an arena to fill, "and they weren't going to do it by having a black team in the heart of the South," said one white player.[50]

The team's media problems also extended to its obvious omission of the African American press. The *Atlanta Daily World*, the city's black newspaper, made occasional announcements about upcoming games, particularly when star black players like the Warriors' Nate Thurmond or the Celtics' Bill Russell were coming to town. Yet the team itself made no effort to advertise in the city's black publications.[51] Through the bulk of the team's first season, the *World*'s sports section exhibited far more interest in football, baseball, and soccer. Even as the Hawks made a playoff run to the Western Conference finals in its first season in Atlanta, the paper generally ignored the team, running only one article about only one postseason game. While Hank Aaron was covered with some regularity, most of the nonwire sports coverage still focused on HBCU contests and other local black sports. Thus the sports page in the black press following the integration of athletics served largely as a supplement to existing coverage in other mainstream papers and news sources.[52]

The Hawks, after all, were playing home games at Georgia Tech prior to building its new arena, the Omni. Tech had yet to integrate, and it was a white space that was generally unwelcoming to the black population. It also featured an all-white collegiate basketball team, and it was hosting a professional team that was whitening for the sake of broader white support.

The team did provide one later advertisement for the black press, one welcoming the doctors of the National Medical Association, the largest group of black doctors in the country. The advertisement was part of a special, surely solicited section in the *Atlanta Daily World*. It included an image of Bill Bridges instead of Pete Maravich, despite the fact that the LSU star was the center of the team's marketing efforts after he was drafted. The ad was not part of the team's regular, broader advertising campaign. Overall, the Hawks enjoyed little coverage and analysis. There was less reporting about the team than there was about black NBA stars like Earl Monroe, Oscar Robertson, Lew Alcindor, and Elgin Baylor. The Hawks received less coverage than Aaron and the Braves, less than soccer and the city's entrant in the North American Soccer League, and less than the professional wrestling championship bouts of Nick Bockwinkel, the Assassin, and others.[53]

In the off-season, the Hawks had the third pick in the draft. Blake later claimed that he wanted Florida State center Dave Cowens, while Guerin remembered wanting Dan Issel from Kentucky. Tom Cousins, however, overruled them both.[54] Cowens and Issel were white southerners, as well, but Cousins was after a white player who performed like a black player. He wanted the Great White Hope.

Even before he bought the Hawks, Cousins attended a basketball game in Athens between the University of Georgia and LSU in January 1968. A sophomore named Pete Maravich amazed the real estate man and everyone else in attendance. When he bought the Hawks, Cousins vowed not to involve himself in basketball decisions, with one notable exception. "I don't know anything about basketball," he told Guerin and Blake, "but if we ever have a shot at this guy Maravich, I want him." Guerin told him that he wasn't sure Maravich would "ever make it in the NBA." That, however, wasn't Cousins's concern: "He'll make the sport in Atlanta, Georgia."[55] The statement contained clear racial calculation, but in all fairness, it also expressed the enthusiasm of someone who had been awed by a singular talent. Or, perhaps, an original enthusiasm over a singular talent developed into a racial calculation that would stimulate business in downtown Atlanta.

Cousins hired Bob Kent to manage the development of the team's arena, and Kent was close to Press Maravich, Pete's father and coach at LSU. The Hawks had the San Francisco Warriors' first-round draft pick because of an earlier trade, and as the Warriors struggled through the 1969–70 season, that pick began looking better and better (as the quality of draft choices was inverse to teams' success the previous season). Anticipating a high-ranking choice, Cousins sent Kent to Baton Rouge to recruit Maravich away from the increasingly powerful ABA. The younger league targeted Pete in his junior year at LSU, ownership deciding that the Carolina Cougars should be the team to draft him. ABA owners understood the draw of white superstars in the South, too, and they were in competition with the NBA far more than with each other. There had been talk among Hawks' executives of making Press Maravich the team's coach, but though that effort fell through, the recruitment of his son never stopped.[56]

After Detroit and San Diego selected Bob Lanier and Rudy Tomjanovich, respectively, the Atlanta Hawks used the third pick in the 1970 NBA draft on Maravich. Guerin was angry. "I found out the night before the draft that we were taking Pete Maravich." Blake was so frustrated that he resigned after sixteen years with the team. The Hawks refused to give Lenny Wilkens a $60,000 contract two years prior, but in 1970 gave "Pistol" Pete a massive deal. It guaranteed the LSU guard $1.5 million for five years, with performance bonuses and a no-trade clause. The Hawks would provide him with his own private secretary, his own apartment, and a new car complete with car phone prior to each season. He also received $50 a month for gas. The contract was $400,000 more than that of Bob Lanier, the top draft pick overall, and it was $500,000 more than that of Lew Alcindor, who had been drafted first the previous season. As a kind of racial damage control, rumors began almost immediately that the signing, though expensive, increased season ticket sales by a third within the first twenty-four hours.[57]

The Hawks had another first-round pick in 1970, using it on white UCLA guard John Vallely, the only player drafted in that year's first round with a negative career win shares statistic.[58] Still on the board when Atlanta took the redundant and mediocre Vallely with the fourteenth pick were future all-star guards Calvin Murphy and Tiny Archibald. "He couldn't play dead," Blake said of Vallely. The Hawks gave him a $300,000 two-year contract nonetheless. Only adding to the tumult, the team used its second-round pick to select Dan Hester, Maravich's teammate at LSU. He wouldn't make the team, instead playing for both the Denver Rockets and Kentucky

Colonels of the ABA during that 1970–71 season. It would be the only year of Hester's professional career.[59]

The addition of Maravich would ultimately mean the subtraction of Joe Caldwell. A loophole in Joe Caldwell's contract allowed him to become a free agent. When the 1970 all-star used that provision as leverage to get a deal more closely resembling the money being paid to the team's unproven white talent, the Hawks demurred. In February 1970, the NBA signed a new three-year contract with ABC, assuring the league a minimum of twenty-eight televised games. "Maravich was pegged as the great white hope of the ball club," Caldwell stated, "as well as its main drawing card." Caldwell ultimately left for the ABA's Carolina Cougars, but he claimed that while negotiating a new deal in the wake of the Maravich signing, Tom Cousins told him very plainly, "One white player is better than six niggers." At that point, Caldwell left the negotiating table and vowed never to play for Atlanta again. He was certainly bitter about his release, and thus had reason to exaggerate, and Cousins never had a reputation as an overt racist. Still, Caldwell felt comfortable with such a public assertion, and the lack of any public denial demonstrates if nothing else the racial state of play within the organization, whether or not the Hawks' owner ever used such a slur during contract negotiations.[60]

Publicly, the players claimed to support the decision. "A white player of his [Maravich's] ability is what Atlanta and the NBA need," Bridges told the media the day after the draft. "He may be the greatest gate attraction to come in the league, and that doesn't hurt. It could mean a couple of hundred thousand dollars to all of us Hawks." Privately, things were more problematic. Because of the situation on the team, with the new white showboat player being paid massively more than the established, successful black veterans, Pete became the scapegoat for every player concern. "It was always Pete's fault," said team statistician Hank Kalb.[61]

Maravich was, if nothing else, a legitimate star. "A loose-limbed, floppy-haired 6-foot-5-inch guard with sagging gray socks as his trademark," as the *New York Times* described him, the LSU guard's style and seemingly endless ability to score turned him into a folk hero. He averaged more than forty-four points per game in college, leading the NCAA for each of his three varsity years. In an age when few collegiate games were televised, and even fewer for relatively poor teams with a relatively slim basketball legacy like LSU, word of his statistical triumphs spread largely without visual evidence. Maravich's play became the stuff of legend because his records were shrouded in the cloak of mystery. That legend, in turn, led to constant discussion, media profiles, and individual television appearances. Even before his massive contract, it was almost a fait accompli that Pete would arrive in the NBA as more than a player. He would arrive as a national sensation.[62]

The Hawks began training camp in Jacksonville on September 17, 1970. Not only did Maravich not perform well, but Guerin also chose to make Herb White, an eighth-round white draft choice from the University of Georgia, an Atlanta Hawk. White made the team over more talented black players. Training camp only drove the racial wedges deeper, rankling Walt Hazzard most of all. (Leadership's constant displays of deference to Maravich threatened Hazzard's spot as a more traditional point guard.) When the season started, White and Maravich became roommates on road trips.[63]

Only exacerbating such problems, Maravich signed endorsement contracts with a variety of companies hungry for a white basketball star. He also turned down a leading movie role. The Hawks' new advertising campaign touted the "New Hawks" despite the fact that the team was the league's defending Western Conference champion. An all-white band played "Dixie" during warm-ups at 1970 home games. That summer, the Hawks moved to the weak Central Division of the Eastern Conference and assumed that even with the defections there was reason for optimism. But there wasn't. The black veterans resented the highly paid Maravich, whose flamboyant passing and play further aggravated resentments about compensation. Meanwhile, the white southern fans were supremely devoted to the Great White Hope, who emphasized their entertainment more than what most would consider team play. "He knew how to play one way," Guerin remembered. "His dad turned him loose at LSU, and that's the only way he knew."[64]

That defending Western Conference champion Hawks team began the season 7-21, and Pete wasn't playing well. Lack of success divided the team into the old guard and the new—essentially the black players and the white. Former NC State player Hal Blondeau was shocked when he saw the Hawks play at Madison Square Garden that season: "It was four black guys and Pete. It was like he wasn't there. They just wouldn't give him the ball." Maravich was, wrote the *Atlanta Constitution*'s Jesse Outlar, "as welcome as George Wallace at a Rockefeller house party."[65]

While the wins no longer came as easily, the economic bottom line was stronger for the change. ABC's *Wide World of Sports* paid $75,000 for broadcasting rights to the Hawks' season opener against the Milwaukee Bucks and added lights to Alexander Memorial Coliseum for the game. Maravich didn't play particularly well, but he was the reason for the show.[66] During the team's first two years in Atlanta, management couldn't sell its local broadcasting rights. During the 1970–71 season, the Hawks played on national television five times. Though the team was much less talented and successful than its predecessors, it sold out thirteen games. Attendance rose by more than 20 percent. Team revenues increased by more than 50 percent. "Without question," said Cousins, "I don't think there would be a new arena if we hadn't gotten Pete Maravich."[67]

The Hawks would have a late-season resurgence, finishing 12-5 with Maravich averaging twenty-nine points per game. The team lost to the Knicks in the first round of the Eastern Conference playoffs, four games to one. And while the Hawks ended the season with a losing record—its first in Atlanta— attendance rose.[68]

The Maravich saga would be a very public demonstration of the racial issues surrounding the first NBA team in the Deep South. But it wouldn't be the most public demonstration. Race problems were inherent in negotiating the insertion of a black team from a black league into a white city for the purpose of gentrifying a downtown neighborhood. Perhaps inevitably, these problems would seep beyond the bounds of the local sports pages.

Upon the team's purchase in May 1968, Tom Cousins announced that he had no inclination to participate in basketball operations. "I don't think Carl [Sanders] is giving up his political activities. We'll have the right man to run things," he told reporters. "We didn't buy the Hawks to make a lot of money."[69] Cousins was right; Sanders had no intention of removing himself from politics and devoting himself to basketball. In 1970, the former Georgia governor decided to run again for his old post. He had served as a racial moderate from 1962 to 1966 in a state that didn't allow successive terms, so despite his popularity he could not run for immediate reelection.[70]

And so replacing Sanders as the racial moderate in 1966 would be the candidate Jimmy Carter. Carter had refused to join the White Citizens' Council as a young man and argued for allowing black worshipers in his hometown church. As a state senator, he had stumped against black voting restrictions. In the 1966 election, Carter refused to exploit race as a political issue, even though it was the most pressing matter of the campaign. He finished a surprisingly successful third place to eventual winner and notorious racist Lester Maddox. This was a significant shift for a state that had seemed to be moving toward racial moderation prior to that election. Adding insult to injury, in 1968, the year the Hawks came to Atlanta, Georgia became one of the Deep South states (along with Alabama, Mississippi, Louisiana, and Arkansas) that voted for George Wallace in the presidential election.[71]

The popularity of Maddox and the vote for Wallace in 1968 undercut the popular assumption in 1967 that Sanders would return triumphant in 1970. White Georgia had taken a hard right turn on race at precisely the time that its new black professional team arrived. In March 1968, 35 percent of Georgians believed integration was moving too fast. In April 1970, that number was 54 percent. Antiblack sentiment in Georgia stood at 10 percent in March 1968 and at 49 percent in April 1970. Carter never left the public eye in the following four years, fully intending to run again in 1970, and he understood that he would need to oppose the former governor from the right in the Democratic primary. Carter couldn't, however, go so far to the racial right that he couldn't return to the center in a general election. So the racial coding of his campaign would need to be subtle, the line he walked incredibly—and necessarily—narrow.[72]

Carter's campaign was one of sound and fury, but though it had no significant policy consistency, it did signify something: white middle- and lower-class frustration—at anything. Generally. If it was the wealthy, the city, a potential scandal, or a potential black take-over, that was fine. Whatever worked. Black voters were already supporting Sanders, so Carter could come to rural whites as a populist, with the inherent understanding that they would know the racial codes with which that came. He recorded a radio commercial where he promised not to be tied to any "bloc" vote. That was racial code for the black vote, but just to be sure he wasn't misunderstood, Carter slurred the word so that it could be heard as "black." His campaign also paid for radio advertisements for black candidate C. B. King in an effort to draw votes away from Sanders. "I expect," said Carter, "to have particularly strong support from the people who voted for George Wallace for president and the ones who voted for Lester Maddox."[73]

Early in the summer of 1970 the Carter campaign released a series of anonymous flyers designed to attack Sanders more directly. One featured Sanders being doused with champagne by two large black men. It was a photo common to those involved in professional sports. The Atlanta Hawks celebrated a division championship by pouring champagne over the heads of teammates, personnel, and ownership. Such was the shorthand of professional athletics, but Georgians outside of the capital had yet to learn that language. The Hawks celebration picture became known as the "champagne shampoo." Campaign officials sent it to rural areas all over the state. It appeared at Ku Klux Klan rallies and at churches. The picture demonstrated Sanders's wealth, his association with alcohol, and, most importantly, his association with blacks. The flyer aided others that highlighted Sanders's association with Julian Bond, the fact that Sanders had attended Martin Luther King's funeral, and Sanders's opposition to George Wallace.[74] Carter's campaign made an effort to use the Hawks—a symbol of black Atlanta—to convince white Georgia that his opponent did not advocate white interests. Professional basketball was in the same category as Julian Bond or Martin Luther King. It wasn't simply foreign. It was antagonistic toward white values.

Ray Abernathy, a former vice president of the Gerald Rafshoon Advertising Agency, credited the Hawks flyer to Carter press secretary Bill Pope. Another Rafshoon vice president, Dorothy Wood, saw the leaflet collected "in groups of several hundred or so in the office." Gerald Rafshoon himself discussed it with Wood over drinks. The *Atlanta Constitution*'s Bill Shipp witnessed Pope passing out the flyer at a Ku Klux Klan rally. "A slightly-built fellow, his hat pulled down over his eyes, quietly circulated through the crowd passing out handbills," wrote Shipp. "'I don't know what it is, but I bet it's good,' said one Kluxer as he grabbed a sheet of paper. It was a photograph of Carl Sanders being doused with champagne by a Negro basketball player."[75]

That Negro basketball player was Bill Bridges, who had arrived with the team from St. Louis and appeared at the Hawks' introductory press conference in May 1968. The picture went to Ku Klux Klan rallies, but also to white Baptist ministers, barbershops, gas stations, and police officers, among others. The flyers came from a post office in Decatur and used a fake committee heading. The campaign team used postage stamps so there could be no tracing the meter number.[76]

"We distributed that leaflet," said Abernathy. "It was prepared by Bill Pope, who was then Carter's press secretary. It was part of an operation we called 'the stink tank.'" Abernathy also claimed that Carter presidential campaign manager Hamilton Jordan masterminded the flyer with Rafshoon. (Both Jordan and Rafshoon denied the allegation.) "Carter's campaign financed King's media advertising," said Abernathy. "I personally prepared all of King's radio ads while I was on Rafshoon's payroll and supervised the production. And I helped channel money to the company Rafshoon used to pay for them. . . . I don't know if Jimmy knew about it, but everyone else did."[77]

Attorney Charles Kirbo, Hamilton Jordan, Gerald Rafshoon, and Bill Pope met most Sundays during the campaign in room 232 of the Quality Central Hotel to discuss strategy, including "the race question." "It was something we joked about in the office," said Abernathy, referring to the Hawks flyer. "At the time, it seemed like a hell of a lot of fun."[78]

"Oh, gosh, they were binding them in groups of several hundred or so in the office," said Dorothy Wood. "I remember seeing several stacks of them. I had a fairly big office then, and I remember that they put several stacks of them in one corner of it for a few days." Though Carter denied involvement with the circular, Reg Murphy, former editor of the *Atlanta Constitution*, was doubtful. "Mr. Carter has been quoted as saying how he didn't know anything about the leaflet prior to its distribution. Technically, that might be true. But not philosophically," Murphy wrote. "He obviously was operating on the basis of 'Don't tell me about it; but get the job done.' The fact is that Mr. Carter—even after he knew about the leaflet—never ordered his people to stop it. And he most certainly never apologized for it."[79]

Carter won the election. Two years later, he would oversee the opening of the Hawks' new arena, the Omni. Four years after that, he would win the presidential election. But the Hawks' appearance in the 1970 gubernatorial race—as the race-baiting pawn of a future president with a consistent track record of racial moderation—demonstrated the power of the black NBA image in the minds of white Georgians, many of whom were experiencing Sunbelt prosperity against their will.

While suffering some initial delays in planning, the Omni's construction progressed with the reasonable alacrity for which the NBA had hoped. Cousins funded the venture without public money, chose the design, and broke ground in March 1971. The coliseum was ready the following year for the opening of the Hawks' season on October 15, 1972. Richie Guerin had moved on, but Maravich remained. He scored twenty-eight points in a win over the Knicks.[80]

Omni, ironically, is Latin for "every." It was a word of inclusion representing a symbol of gentrification. As part of the development plan, Cousins continued building the Omni International, a massive office and convention complex near the arena. Opening in 1976, the International was part of the developer's attempt at reinvigorating the downtown area. Initially, however, it didn't work. As the Hawks struggled and their arena remained mostly empty, so too did the complex associated with it. That season, the Hawks finished twenty games under .500 and had the lowest attendance in the league, as the original allure of the white savior gave way to fans' frustration with the team's lack of success. The Hawks would have two strong seasons in 1978 and 1979, but their first sustained success since the racial dismantling of the late 1960s would begin in the 1985–86 season. The University of Georgia's Dominique Wilkins, who played his best basketball since being drafted in 1982, led that team. Wilkins was local and exciting, and he normalized blackness for Atlanta's white fan base. The previous season, Wilkins had won the NBA's slam dunk contest. In 1986, he lost to his teammate, the diminutive point guard Spud Webb. Along with Doc Rivers, Kevin Willis, Tree Rollins, and others, a group of predominantly black players led by a former Bulldog known as the "Human Highlight Film" would help make basketball more palatable to the city.[81]

In 1987, CNN moved its headquarters to the Omni International, and the development changed its name to the CNN Center. The year after CNN's move, Sanders's original prediction finally came true. The Democratic National Convention came to the Omni to nominate Massachusetts governor Michael Dukakis for president.[82] Thus the team whose residency in the Deep South began with racial politics surrounding its best player, Lenny Wilkens, finally found a measure of acceptance twenty years later with the absence of racial politics surrounding its best player, Dominique Wilkins.

The late 1960s and early 1970s heralded a broader critique of the traditional notion that sports was a character-building endeavor. Each in its own way, Russell's autobiography in 1966, Harry Edwards's *The Revolt of the Black Athlete* in 1969, Dave Meggyesy's *Out of Their League* and Jim Bouton's *Ball Four* in 1970, and Jack Scott's *The Athletic Revolution* in 1971 gave the lie to the myth that sports was a cure for society's ills. At the same time, however, the likes of Richard Nixon, Spiro Agnew, and Ronald Reagan marshaled sports as a check against such countercultural messages. That check coincided with a rise of sports in the Sunbelt, as new cities in the expanding South and West sought to burnish their reputations with professional teams. In turn, those teams would, at least in the popular mind, take on the conservative values of those cities.[83]

The Hawks' move to Atlanta initially problematized that transition by placing a black team from a black league into the heart of the Deep South at a time of significant racial unrest. Still, following a business model that played not to its employees but to the racial assumptions of its clientele, Hawks management steadily eroded the talent of the team in order to make it more palatable to conservative Sunbelt values. Or, as David Halberstam surmised, Atlanta's management, "anxious not to offend its white fans (or, more accurately, hoping to locate them), had broken up a very successful, virtually all-black team, and drafted Maravich out of college." That being the case, "primarily for racial reasons, [Atlanta] remained a troubled franchise for a decade to come."[84]

But the simple fact that race was a contributing factor in the Hawks' demise demonstrated, as did the gubernatorial election of 1970, that it wasn't just the franchise that was troubled. Atlanta was situated at several fraught intersections: It was a city that wooed a successful professional sports team, only to ruin that success for the sake of race. It was a city that purchased a black team from a black league in order to gentrify a struggling black downtown area. And it was a city cloaked in a self-image laden with color-blind, business-minded motives and a hunger for civic growth that was still hoping to build Margaret Mitchell Square Garden. If that metaphor was a stand-in for a crumbling edifice that represented Old South values in the face of racial progress, decimated by hubris and ultimately bound to take the humble shape that modernity dictated for it, then Margaret Mitchell Square Garden is exactly what Atlanta got.

4 SAMBO'S BOYS

Sam Battistone was the son of Italian immigrants, coal miners who wanted a better life for their son. By the 1930s, Battistone had made good and was running a diner in downtown Santa Barbara, California, but he saw greater opportunity. He teamed with partner Newell Bohnett to create a new restaurant chain in 1957. Taking Battistone's first name and the first part of Bohnett's surname, the pair named their new business Sambo's and decorated it with pictures based on Helen Bannerman's 1899 *The Story of Little Black Sambo*. Menu items were named after characters in the story, and nothing was done to hide the inherent racism in such depictions. Instead, the restaurant played them up. From that first restaurant in Santa Barbara came another in Sacramento. Battistone's son, Sam Battistone Jr., led much of the expansion. Two years later, six restaurants served customers in California. By 1963 there were twenty in business on the West Coast. A decade later, in 1972, there were 257 across the country, and by 1974 there were hundreds more.[1]

In each new restaurant, Sambo iconography adorned the walls and menus. As the restaurants spread across the South in the 1960s and 1970s, a South still in the grips of a civil rights movement and often offended by the racist depictions hovering over their pancakes and coffee, Sambo's seemed doomed to eventual failure. An American past of overt racism and capitalist overexpansion played on the eventual success of the franchise, which would ultimately declare bankruptcy in 1982. When Battistone Jr. decided to finance a professional basketball team and place it in New Orleans, part of that evolving Sunbelt South, the team he created would ultimately suffer the same fate in the region as did his restaurant chain. The history of racism in the southern reception of professional basketball and the NBA's expansion into a market that had proven unready for the sport ultimately doomed the franchise briefly known as the New Orleans Jazz.

Race undoubtedly played a role in the demise of the Jazz, as it had in the dismantling of the Hawks, but such was not the team's principal failing. Nor had race been the principal failing of the city's ABA predecessor, the Buccaneers, though it had clearly played a role. Ultimately, the histories of the Deep South's first NBA team and its first ABA team shaped the Jazz. Racism and the foreignness of a "black sport" like professional basketball, then, combined with an overexuberant civic ideal that sought a place for New Orleans in the burgeoning Sunbelt by bringing in professional sports to bolster a reputation the city was not ready to embrace. It was largely an overreach in an attempt to erase the reputation of a racist past that combined with the real residue of that racism to become the final curtain of the city's first NBA experiment. That a California Mormon with no intention of coming to the South and an infamously racist restaurant chain financed the first act did not portend the last-act success that the team and the city hoped to achieve.

In early March 1974, Baton Rouge lawyer Sheldon Beychok, former executive counsel to Gov. Edwin Edwards, and Beverly Hills lawyer and agent Fred Rosenfeld met with the NBA's expansion committee in Chicago as part of the Battistone retinue to pitch New Orleans as an NBA city. "I am very, very optimistic and quite confident all will go well," said Beychok. Battistone, for his part, had never built a restaurant in the city. Rosenfeld explained that the group chose New Orleans after commissioning a study by the Stanford Research Institute on the best possible places for a team. "The key [factor] in convincing us New Orleans was a good choice was the [survey]," he said.

"It pointed to the Superdome as a drawing attraction and pointed to the success of sports in other domed stadiums."[2]

Meanwhile, the league meetings also included discussions about generating new teams through merger. The ABA, which had already left New Orleans and its Buccaneers behind, was discussing consolidation to possibly four or six teams in an effort to make a merger more likely. "Consolidation is the key," explained Roy Boe, president of the ABA's New York Nets. "Our franchises are certainly better candidates for expansion than any new cities the NBA could consider." It was a direct shot at New Orleans, which had failed as an ABA city. NBA commissioner Walter Kennedy appeared at least marginally receptive to such arguments, only expanding the potential obstacles to the city's bid.[3]

Beychok's optimism, however, would prevail over merger politics. The NBA's March meeting included no decisions about a union with the ABA, but a nine-person ownership group won the NBA's eighteenth franchise for New Orleans for $6.15 million. Joining Battistone, Rosenfeld, and Beychok were Andrew Martin, chair of the state mineral board, Baton Rouge businessmen Jules LeBlanc and J. J. McKernan, California businessmen Jerrold Rabin and Fred H. Miller, and Biloxi's Robert Bell. The association established an expansion draft for the new team and planned to include it for the new season beginning in October. "We expect to move very quickly now," said Rosenfeld.[4] At a press conference the following day, he promised a competitive team. "If we have proper management and coaching and can draft the kind of people you would employ in any of your businesses, I think we will be competitive."[5]

The windfall raised the expectations of the city. The *States-Item*'s Scott Slonim was confident after the NBA acquisition that "the city is about to embark on what in all probability will be its last baseball season without a major league franchise to call its own." While major-league baseball never materialized in New Orleans, Slonim's surety spoke to the city's confidence in its Sunbelt legitimacy. "You would have to describe the first local exposure of Fred Rosenfeld," said Peter Finney, "as impressive."[6]

While there was some optimism in response to the new franchise, there was also worry. Former Buccaneers executive Maurie Stern knew what fan apathy looked like, and he knew that it hadn't gone away. "I know the NBA has a lot of prestige to it," he claimed, "but I was disappointed . . . when we had UCLA and North Carolina State here in the Sugar Bowl [basketball tournament], and the Auditorium was half empty." Such was not to say that Stern did not want the new professional team to succeed. "New Orleans deserves a franchise. I hope it makes it. I'm certainly going to be behind them." The massive new stadium known as the Superdome, built principally for the city's NFL franchise, would surely help. "They will have a better location and better parking than we had. That worked against us. They don't have that to worry about." Ben Levy, executive director of the Superdome Commission, was just as enthusiastic. So, too, was University of New Orleans head coach Ron Greene. Both of them pointed to the Dome as the most important difference for the city's second chance at pro basketball.[7]

The *Louisiana Weekly*, the city's black newspaper, diligently reported on the creation of the expansion franchise. "The reason—?" sports editor Jim Hall asked. "The Louisiana Superdome is the answer." That, too, was a potential problem for black New Orleans. In the same column, Hall announced, "It is very important that all races regardless of color, be a part of the working force within the Dome." Like everyone else, Hall was overawed by the Superdome, sure that with the new stadium, "New Orleans will start its big move towards becoming a big time sports center." But the legacy of the Buccaneers was still close-by. No matter what big events or professional sports the Dome attracted, "it is the general public in the New Orleans Area and elsewhere that will have to support 'em."[8]

The Superdome was a key component to the city's NBA offer, though it would not be open until the team's second season. The venue always came with attendant controversy. A day after the NBA's New Orleans announcement, owners held a public press conference in the city. Meanwhile, state senator Nat G. Kiefer, head of a legislative committee charged with investigating the Dome's problematic construction, admitted to leading a group of "local investors" planning on buying a minority stake in the team. "I do not want to give the wrong impression, it is not a firmed-up deal where the money has been put up. But it is a group of men willing to do it," he said. "We've had, I guess, three or four meetings." To make the transaction sound even shadier, he made an ardent promise to a *Times-Picayune* reporter: "If we had the money in the bank, I would tell you exactly who it is [in the investment group]. But I can tell you this, you know, it is in the business community." As head of his Superdome investigatory committee, Kiefer had recently charged that the 1971 state legislature had been "misled" by a bond ceiling placed on Dome financing. A month later, he took credit for the bond ceiling measure and claimed that it saved the stadium. Such was the nature of Louisiana politics. Such was also the danger of including politicians with a vested interest in the Superdome and a track record of duplicity as part of the team's ownership group.[9]

It was a relationship made only more problematic two days later when the team provided the Superdome Commission a letter of intent for a ten-year lease. The Jazz promised the venue $2,000 per game or 8 percent of gross ticket sales for the first five seasons, that number rising to 10 percent for the second five. The Superdome would also retain all income from concessions, parking, and stadium advertising, dramatically limiting the team's ability to generate revenue. In addition, the franchise would pay for all ticket sellers and takers, ushers, security, cleaning staff, scoreboard operators, and any other game employees, with an additional 5 percent on top of those costs as an administrative fee to the Superdome. "We don't know what the NBA franchise will charge for tickets or what they will have in paid attendance," said commission executive director Ben Levy. Even so, the deal would ensure that the venue would still turn a profit from the team's games. He explained that the new stadium would have eighteen thousand "excellent seats" and thirty-five thousand "really acceptable seats" for basketball, numbers beyond what any other NBA venue held or any other NBA team averaged. The deal did not seem to take any lessons from the Buccaneers' struggles, nor did it augur well for the Jazz's success. It was a deal, more than anything else, designed to benefit the Superdome.[10]

"In this era of planned obsolescence, the Superdome is the ultimate obsoletor," opined Jep Cadou in the *Saturday Evening Post*. "Like a giant button mushroom built near the Mississippi upon bayou swampland and set against the delta skyline, it looms majestically over streets named Bourbon and Basin and Desire—the perfect rebuttal to Houston's decade-old Astrodome."[11] The

Dome was scheduled to open in May 1975, but as early as January, Levy sent a confidential letter to the architect expressing grave doubt as to the optimistic deadline. Sure enough, in February Levy announced that mid-June was the next best chance. The city's Superdome Commission was dismayed. Who could provide a definitive open date? "I believe that's the Lord now," responded Jefferson Parish president Thomas Donelon. "We don't know." If the stadium wasn't completed by May 1 as originally projected, promised an angry Donelon, the commission would sue the contractors.[12]

By late March, the projected completion date had been moved to August 1, but Levy reassured the city and the state: "Tulane and the Saints must be accommodated in that facility for a full season of football. Let there be no question about that in anybody's mind." Perhaps the Dome would still be in need of minor adjustments, but at the very least, it would be football ready. Meanwhile, construction costs topped $178 million, and the Superdome Commission was anxious about the Dome's ability to pay for itself. Both the Saints and Green Wave signed contracts to play their football games in the stadium. However, estimated revenue projections hinted that the Dome would need to generate an average of $30,000 a day to remain in the black. The Jazz, then, would be paramount in allowing the stadium to keep its financial head above water.[13]

May passed. Then June. But as August approached, officials were confident that the building would be ready to open. In contrast New Orleans residents were flummoxed by the controversy, the cost, and the delays. They remained skeptical of the bizarre monstrosity now peeking out of the downtown skyline. "No wonder we're getting reports about all those UFOs," remarked one doubtful cabdriver. "They're flying around that thing because they think it's their mother."[14]

For the team's first season prior to the Dome's completion, Municipal Auditorium manager Richie Dixon was "licking his chops at the $1900 to $2000 rental per night the auditorium will reap." Municipal's more modest but realistic capacity was 8,000, with 7,500 "good seats." The team would play most of its games in Municipal and its others at Loyola's Field House, which had hosted the Buccaneers in the decade prior.[15]

"Professional basketball is coming to New Orleans and will be played in Loyola's Fieldhouse," the school's newspaper reported. "Sound like a seven year old announcement of the now forgotten New Orleans Buccaneers of the American Basketball Association?" The *Maroon* assured its readers that it was not. The new team, "as yet unnamed," would play at the field house several times in January and February. "We're just a backup facility," explained Loyola's intramural director. Municipal Auditorium would be the team's regular pre-Superdome home, the team moving to the university "when they have a conflict because of Mardi Gras balls or something."[16]

The team's broadcaster, Rodney "Hot Rod" Hundley, was unimpressed. The Loyola Field House "had a tin roof and it sounded like machine gun fire when it rained. The court was on a stage, and they had a net around the court to keep players from falling off the stage. I announced games from an orchestra pit on the side of the court." Even though the setup only allowed for several thousand fans, "we still couldn't sell the games out."[17] The Buccaneers had been very familiar with this problem. The *Maroon* sports editor wondered if the team could survive, recalling the city's failed ABA experiment. "In one game, in fact, the players, coaches and officials outnumbered the fans." Still, the author argued, this new team would soon occupy the Superdome, a far superior facility to Loyola's "damp, heatless concrete." Moreover, the Jazz would do so in the NBA, a more established league with a reputation that would better draw fans.[18]

To fill Municipal Auditorium and Loyola's Field House, not to mention the Superdome, team executives realized they needed players that Louisiana wanted to see. Or at least a player. "The demise of the ABA Buccaneers is a tombstone which marks the fact that a successful franchise is [about] more than winning basketball," warned the *Times-Picayune*'s Larry McMillen. "Winning helps, but a successful ticket selling job is the key." That job fell to Barry Mendelson, the team's vice president of business operations. "Boiled down to its simplest," wrote McMillen, "he is the man who must sell professional basketball to football-oriented New Orleanians." Mendelson promised that the team would have no "splashy uniforms, hokey promotions, or bad halftime shows." He promised, disingenuously, as it turned out, "Nothing we do will be garish."[19]

Most important, however, was a star performer. To that end, they eyed the Great White Hope that had come to Atlanta four years prior from LSU. "I told Pistol that he should leave Atlanta and go to New Orleans," said the Knicks' Walt Frazier. "I told him he could be a king there, but he says he doesn't think the NBA will go over in New Orleans."[20] That did not stop New Orleans from courting him, and from offering Atlanta much of its capital and future draft picks for the privilege. New Orleans was not even among the top thirty-five American media outlets, making it an unlikely choice for an NBA franchise, particularly after the city's ABA experiment. "We didn't have the population base that could support forty-one home games— unless we had something special," Mendelson explained. "Pete Maravich was that specialness. We were bringing home the favorite son. He became a promotional and marketing imperative."[21]

Maravich's tenure in Atlanta had been a mix of success and failure. Most recently, however, he had experienced failure. The Hawks had missed the playoffs the previous season, and Maravich had been suspended briefly for a verbal altercation with Atlanta coach Cotton Fitzsimmons. He had even discussed an early retirement after his current contract ended, feeling that the organization had scapegoated him for the team's poor performance. At the very least, Maravich was a player with baggage. Leveraging the team's future drafts for such an athlete simply could not have happened if Pete had not been a white star from LSU.[22]

Meanwhile, a deal could only happen if Maravich, who had a no-trade clause in his contract, agreed to it, and the curmudgeonly star refused to commit, though he clearly did not want to remain in Atlanta. "I won't make any comment at all," he said, "until I talk with my attorneys and others concerned." But "I really can't tolerate any more deceit and deception on the part of the [Atlanta] coach and present administration." Meanwhile, New Orleans native Jimmy Jones, a black guard from Utah's ABA Stars and a New Orleans native, publicly lobbied for the opportunity to play for his hometown's new team. "It's understandable that New Orleans would want him [Maravich]," posited one NBA coach. "But I wouldn't think they would want to sink their future in him. He will put people in the stands, but a guard like Jones will put 'Ws' in the standings." At the time of those late April discussions, Jones was leading his Utah team, based in Salt Lake City, past the defending champion Indiana Pacers in the ABA's Western Division playoffs.[23]

Ultimately, Maravich's frustration with Atlanta management led him to approve the deal and sign with New Orleans, making him the franchise's first player. The Great White Hope was the prodigal son returning to Louisiana to resurrect professional basketball in the state. In the words of biographer Mark Kriegel, "Even more than a championship, the erstwhile child star wanted to feel loved again."[24] Maravich arrived in early May, but his price tag shocked many. The *Times-Picayune*'s Will Peneguy claimed that the new franchise "turned a $3 phone call in early March into one of the most expensive investments in professional sports." The NBA's other Deep South team, the team that had originally overspent on Maravich, received New Orleans's first-round draft selections for 1974 and 1975, its second-round selections for 1975 and 1976, the second and third picks in the New Orleans expansion draft, and the right to switch first-round selections in 1976 and 1977. By that time, Rosenfeld argued in defense of the lopsided deal, "I honestly feel we'll be ahead of the Hawks in the standings." There was no specific reason for such optimism, but both sides seemed happy. "If New Orleans called the Knicks and offered the same deal for Walt Frazier," explained Atlanta general manager Pat Williams, selling his own city on the loss of its white star, "I'd have to feel the Knicks would have jumped at the deal."[25]

Fans seemed to agree, claiming that the price was "way too much to pay for anybody." The *Times-Picayune*'s Dave Legarde lampooned the deal as the "Louisiana Purchase II." Perhaps "it wasn't as big as its 1815 [sic] predecessor, when the United States stole most of the South and Midwest from France for a meager $15 million, but the reactionaries feel that despite the growing problems of present day gun legislation, New Orleans paid an exorbitant price for its 'Pistol.'" In other words, the team hadn't paid a price, it had paid a "ransom fee." Such was not the impression that team management was hoping to make upon entering the New Orleans market. Peneguy called Rosenfeld "the greatest thing to happen to the city of Atlanta since Sherman left town."[26]

The Maravich deal seemed a bridge too far for the *Louisiana Weekly*'s Jim Hall, as the team was prepared to sacrifice at least two first-round draft choices for the Great White Hope. "The Saints made a mistake like this, prior to their maiden season," wrote Hall, referring to the city's NFL franchise, "and they paid for it." When the deal was eventually complete, Hall was no more encouraged. "Bartender, give us a double shot of Wild Turkey, we need it after last week's deal, which could be one of the most expensive investments in professional sports."[27]

Peter Finney had always been an enthusiastic supporter of Maravich, but even he was skeptical. "My first impression—and my second—is the price was too high." But he also questioned the deal for Atlanta, citing letters from angry fans who had lost their Great White Hope. "I find it incredible to read the Hawks are thinking of trading Maravich," went one such missive. "I had never been to a professional basketball game until he came to Atlanta, but, after seeing him play, it became my favorite sport."[28]

Trading prominent draft choices, however, was deadly to an expansion team. Those picks ultimately became David Thompson and Alex English. (Atlanta was unable to take advantage of its choices, however, as Thompson chose the ABA, and the Hawks traded English to the Milwaukee Bucks.) In addition, one of the team's vice presidents, Barry Mendelson, who had been an agent for Gail Goodrich, convinced the team to trade a future first-round selection to the Lakers for his former charge. The Jazz got thirty-three-year-old Goodrich, and the Lakers got a draft choice that ultimately became Magic Johnson. "They were so far in the hole," explained Hundley, "they were never going to get out."[29]

It was the story of the white South in microcosm, sacrificing economic self-interest for the sake of white supremacy, in this case the supposed supremacy of one white player who the team hoped would bring revenue to compensate for the mismanaged deal. It was also the story of white southern pro basketball in microcosm, as the Hawks had made a similar move in signing Maravich out of college. Thus, in an effort to right the wrongs of the ABA's Buccaneers, the new NBA team secured a permanent though overly expensive venue and a permanent though overly expensive white star. The Jazz, however, forgot that expenses had ultimately doomed its predecessor. "Before the first dribble of the first practice, New Orleans has quickly become an NBA city," wrote the *Times-Picayune*'s Tom Gage. "In feeling, in spirit, in controversy. Trade for a Maravich and people WILL notice."[30]

After securing Maravich, the Jazz began shoring up its front office. Newly hired executives included LSU alums Pat Screen, a former quarterback for the football team, and Bud Johnson, the school's sports information director. The team's coach would also be a Louisiana product. Scotty Robertson, former coach at Byrd High School in Shreveport and current coach at Louisiana Tech, was not exactly a high-profile hire, but he was a Louisiana hire. Rosenfeld had argued that "we were not going to get" Red Holtzman or Bill Sharman.[31] The team could have acquired someone with NBA experience, but team executives were aware of their absentee status and wanted to make local connections where they could, even at the expense of qualifications and experience.

Rosenfeld had represented Lakers Pat Riley, Gail Goodrich, and Elgin Baylor. Battistone was a vocal Lakers fan. Laker scout Bill Bertka brought the two together for an expansion bid. "The expansion team," explained *Los Angeles Times* sports reporter Mark Heisler, "was like a Cub Scout pack to the Lakers Eagle Scouts." Bertka would ultimately become the first Jazz general manager. Among others, he hired Elgin Baylor, who had stood against racism and segregation during his career, as assistant coach.[32]

The team hired another former Laker, Hot Rod Hundley, as its broadcaster. A frustrated Hundley, however, was unimpressed with what he called "the filthiest city I had ever seen." The team's organization was not much better. Hundley explained that the team had hired former LSU quarterback Pat Screen as a vice president, largely because of his New Orleans connections rather than any legitimate knowledge about basketball. "That's the way things were when the Jazz started out." Among the team's largely California ownership group were Baton Rouge lawyer Sheldon Beychok and Thibodeaux oil and real estate man Andrew Martin. Still, Battistone, Bertka, and others never actually moved to the city, and the vacuum that absenteeism created meant chaos at the top of the organization. Funds quickly dwindled, and Battistone relied on his father's money to supplement the team's needs. The team was "run in those days like everyone was on vacation," said Hundley. "I knew right away that the Jazz were doomed in New Orleans."[33]

The organization established its offices in room 617 at the Braniff Place Hotel on Canal Street.[34] That became home base for the team's expansion draft. Each existing franchise was allowed to protect seven players, and New Orleans was able to choose from the rest of their rosters. The squad began by choosing the Chicago Bulls' white center Dennis Awtrey, who was known less for his play and more for infamously punching Kareem Abdul-Jabbar on national television. After making two picks for Atlanta as part of the Maravich deal, the team then selected Jim Barnett, a white guard from Golden State. The team's fourth and fifth picks were John Block and Barry Clemens, another white center and white guard, respectively. In between those pairs, New Orleans selected Walt Bellamy from Atlanta. A black athlete with a history of playing for a southern team, Bellamy was prepared to deal with the racial mores attendant with being in the South.[35]

Thus the first six members of the new team included five white players and a black player from Atlanta. One of them was from LSU, and another was notorious for assaulting a Black Muslim. While the strategy was clearly designed as part of "a successful ticket selling job," the problem was that Bellamy and Maravich decidedly did not get along. This point of friction was one of the reasons Maravich wanted out of Atlanta. While the majority of the team's remaining picks were black players, the play to race as a function of fan support had clearly been a lesson hard learned from the Hawks' survival and the Buccaneers' failure. Using identity politics as a draft strategy left at least the white parts of the city optimistic. If Maravich played well and the draft choices worked out, one New Orleans journalist observed, "our nameless professional basketball team might get off on the right foot."[36]

The team had no first-round choice in the NBA's collegiate draft, after sacrificing it for Maravich, but its first pick, taking place in the second round, was Aaron James. The New Orleans native had played at Grambling and was the leading scorer in the NCAA's small-college division. Also during the draft, Scott Robertson was officially announced as the team's coach. "So what's a man who coached high school teams at Rodessa, La., doing in a place like the NBA?" asked *Times-Picayune* sports editor Bob Roesler. "Was it like a barefoot country boy visiting New York for the first time?"[37]

A week later, in early June, the barefoot country boy's team had a name—
the winner of a citywide naming contest, the Jazz, was chosen by a local
stockbroker and officially adopted. The team's accompanying purple, gold,
and green colors were the colors of Mardi Gras. Jazz was "a great art form
which belongs to New Orleans and its rich history," Rosenfeld explained.
"Jazz can be defined as 'collective improvisation,' and that would also be an
appropriate description of NBA basketball at its best."[38]

Later that month, the NBA held its annual meetings in New Orleans,
where the association was expected to choose a new commissioner to
replace the retiring Walter Kennedy. The acrimonious meetings failed to
elect his replacement, and the league eventually waited a year before hiring Larry O'Brien. Moreover, the association rejected another proposed
merger with the fledgling ABA. The conferences also highlighted one of New
Orleans's biggest hindrances to NBA success. Mardi Gras celebrations occu-
pied Municipal Auditorium for a month during the season and made home
games virtually impossible for the Jazz. Adding to the various aggravations,
Walt Bellamy, whom the Jazz had acquired from Atlanta, retired in frustration with his new team. "New Orleans surely didn't want my services but
because of the Pete Maravich deal they had to take me," said Bellamy, who
was part of the friction with Maravich in Atlanta. "It was all a big con game
on the part of the Hawks."[39]

However, a distinct affinity existed between the Jazz and the Hawks.
"What we face in the Southeast is a tremendous marketing process,"
explained Atlanta general manager Pat Williams. He called that process
"one of education." Knowing that the two teams were in similar situations,
Williams advised, "Time and patience are important, and I think those are
the most important factors for the New Orleans fans to remember. I won't
say that pro basketball can become the vital influence in the Southeast that
football is, but it can take its rightful place."[40]

By August, construction and financing delays dismantled the team's
original plan to move in to the Superdome halfway through its first season. As architects testified in front of a special legislative commission, the
Jazz stewed. "I have been assured on four different occasions by Dome contractors that basketball could be played in the stadium by February 1," said

Rosenfeld. "We are the only tenants the Dome has. The commission has an obligation to us." But the commission didn't feel that obligation. New Orleans mayor Moon Landrieu chaired the state's Superdome Commission, and he publicly doubted a commission vote that would approve the team's playing in the Superdome during its inaugural season.[41]

In September, the Jazz officially announced the hiring of Elgin Baylor as assistant coach, the same Elgin Baylor who stood on the barricade at the intersection of professional basketball and civil rights in Charleston, West Virginia, in 1959. "Basketball is my life," Baylor explained. "I have been offered several head coaching jobs—some in the NBA, the ABA and in college—but this is the first organization that has really impressed me." Baylor also claimed the team's "philosophy is much like mine insofar as running an NBA team goes." Rosenfeld, who had formerly represented Baylor during his playing days, was thrilled. "We are in the basketball business," he said in defense of the choice, "and the best way to develop basketball players is to have the finest personnel to develop those players."[42]

Such is not to say that Baylor had compromised his racial principles in any way. He hated his owner's restaurant chain and told Battistone that he "took a baseball bat" to a Sambo's sign in Washington, DC. "I knocked that damn thing down."[43] Other Battistone signs were less offensive. Placards on public transportation throughout the city pronounced, "The Jazz bounces in two months." To develop statewide enthusiasm for the new team, the Jazz played exhibition games in Monroe and Shreveport before returning to New Orleans for a charity game against the Cleveland Cavaliers for Big Brothers of Greater New Orleans. "This could be the best expansion team in NBA history," the *Loyola Maroon* predicted.[44]

It was decidedly not. The Jazz began its inaugural season on a four-game road trip before returning to Municipal Auditorium. The team lost all of its road games, and it lost its home opener as well, starting the season 0-5. The game featured Dejan's Olympia Brass Band and a performance by trumpet player Al Hirt. Mayor Moon Landrieu and Commissioner Walter Kennedy, forced to stay on the job another year after the association's owners had failed to elect a replacement, were also in attendance. Announced attendance at that first contest was 6,450, a respectable showing for a stadium that seated 8,000, but a portent of future problems when the team moved to an arena that held tens of thousands.[45]

The poor attendance did not improve as the Jazz struggled through a 23-59 season. Scotty Robertson lasted fifteen games, fired after a 1-14 start and replaced by Butch Van Breda Kolff, "a hard-drinking, cigar-chomping ex-Marine." On top of everything else, despite Maravich's flamboyant play, he "struggled emotionally and physically with knee injuries, alcohol, and psychological problems," none helped by his return to Louisiana. In addition, the team faced substantial difficulties. The Jazz signed a deal with local television channel WDSU to broadcast ten away games. However, the telecasts that first season demonstrated the team's marketing problem. Bud Johnson, the club's public relations director, remembered the first game as being heavy on public service announcements and light on paying advertisements: "All the diseases were represented: the Cancer Society, American Heart Association, leukemia. But there was not one commercial minute in that telecast. That's how much interest there was in pro basketball."[46]

The team's struggles translated to financial losses of between $1.5 and $2.0 million in its first season, only exacerbating the owners' difficulty in making the $800,000 annual payment to cover the Jazz's $6.1 million expansion fee. Thus the team petitioned the association in April 1975 to make its annual payment in installments. Rumors had circulated that the team was going to ask the association to assume operation of the franchise as a result of its financial problems. Jazz executives denied the claim, banking on a new installment plan and the opening of the Superdome for the 1975–76 season. "In the best tradition of Mark Twain," Peneguy reported, "claims of the financial death of the New Orleans Jazz have been exaggerated. The patient may have been suffering but is by no means dead."[47]

To alleviate the massive financial burden, the Jazz decided to create a public investment program to generate revenue from locals, offering a 25 percent ownership stake in the Jazz in $100 increments and hoping to raise $2.5 million. Executives quickly assured the public that the stock offer was not a "life or death proposition" for the team, but they simultaneously admitted that "investment should not be made with the idea of a fast financial return." Instead, the sale "should be considered a fun investment," said Lee Reid, the program's coordinator. "It's good for kids. It's fun to go down there and say, 'That's my team down there.'"[48] The sale was a stopgap measure at best, and it could never raise the desired amount, considering that the team could not draw seven thousand fans to home games. "Investment in basketball is not what I would call a wise stock market move," Mendelson reflected after the gimmick's failure. "It's a civic-support, emotional-support type of investment." The only way to make such an investment successful was to actually have strong civic and emotional support to begin with, a support the Jazz struggled to maintain. "Lest we forget," wrote the *Times-Picayune*'s financial writer, Gil Webre, "the New Orleans Basketball Club is designed to be (hopefully and eventually) a money-making outfit."[49]

Making money was not happening. After the move to the cavernous Superdome, said Hundley, "we were giving away tickets like mad." The team would sell tickets in bulk to local businesses for fifty cents to give away to customers as promotions. "We would get 35,000 people at a game, but 25,000 would be in the balcony for 50 cents apiece."[50] To draw in fans and create more interest, the team featured Elena Tatum, who led a second-line Mardi Gras band through the stadium and put voodoo curses on opposing players. The Jazz also held various giveaways and contests for shirts, watches, and even cars. If the team scored 110 points during home games, ticket stubs earned patrons free French fries at Burger King.[51]

Such gimmicks were palliative but not curative. The Jazz lost an additional $1 million dollars during the 1976–77 season and was projected to lose another $1.3 million in the 1977–78 campaign, largely the result of poor attendance and the team's prohibitive contract with the now-operative Superdome. Management of the Dome was the responsibility of Superdome Services Incorporated (SSI), a predominantly black organization that relied heavily on mayor Moon Landrieu to get and sustain its contract. "It is," said SSI executive Don Hubbard, "the first time to my knowledge that minorities on a large scale have had the assurance they can go to their own people for a job . . . and be treated with dignity."[52]

SSI carried an exclusive contract to provide maintenance, fire control, event preparation, ticket sales, tours, and security. The company did not submit the low bid, and legislative and executive officials were charging it with incompetence in sweeping public pronouncements. Some, like Louisiana attorney general William Guste, were claiming that the contract was invalid because it was a creature of Landrieu's patronage. The claims' racial motivation seemed obvious to Hubbard and SSI president Sherman Copelin. Various interests were trying to tear the company down, and, as a *Times-Picayune* writer stated, "Unfortunately, those interests have used race as one of the basic innuendoes, playing on the prejudice that because SSI is predominantly black, it is shiftless and incompetent."[53] This was, after all, a football stadium, and everything about Louisiana football seemed tinged with racial controversy.

The problem for SSI was that—though race almost certainly played a role in the attacks—incompetence seemed to be the norm. New Orleans Jazz basketball fans, for example, had reported pigeon-droppings and syrup on their seats. Landrieu responded by calling for patience: "General Motors didn't start overnight. US Steel didn't either. They didn't reach that level the first day they went into business." Things would be no different, he argued, if the SSI employees were as white as the patrons. "For some reason we aren't quite that tolerant when it comes to involving minorities for the first time in a major kind of industry."[54]

In early November 1975, as the Jazz's second season was getting under way, the commission held a massive meeting in the Superdome. Its decision not to launch an official investigation of SSI was tempered by its refusal to yield the floor to a black SSI employee who asked to speak on the organization's behalf. Even in its most protectionist stance, Superdome leadership appeared racist.[55] Regardless, everyone agreed that SSI wasn't living up to its contract. Gov. Edwin Edwards called for an investigatory panel to assess the stadium's management. Officials in the state government, led by Attorney General Guste, called loudly for the ouster of Copelin and Hubbard. The SSI management team responded by claiming that allegations against them were "racist." It was a standoff made all the more dire by the fact that both sides seemed to have a legitimate beef.[56]

But on November 15, the critics' complaint gained credibility when a ten-year-old boy was mugged in the stadium during Tulane's football game with North Carolina. The Superdome was largely vacant, most of the Green Wave fans choosing to attend an intramural game at Tulane Stadium in protest of the facility's management and the university's contract with the venue. But even with the reduced workload, the SSI guard on the scene refused to help. "This happens all the time," he told the boy's father. The guard made no report and failed to notify police. On top of that, new allegations surfaced that both Copelin and Hubbard had received massive illegal payoffs from the now-defunct Family Health Foundation.[57]

Officials convened a special advisory committee to evaluate Dome management. Emmett Douglas, state president of the NAACP, sat on the board. "One thing the public can be sure of is that there will by no means be a whitewash," he told reporters. "I will be one member of the committee that will call a spade a spade." Douglas was a competent state leader, but that wasn't why he was chosen. His appointment, and the appointment of Dillard University's Charles Teamer, was designed to counteract potential charges of racism in committee affairs.[58]

"Some appropriate means must be found to get the Louisiana Superdome out of the politics that is threatening to destroy it," argued an editorial in the New Orleans *Times-Picayune*. "The public will not bear the confessed ineptitude and deficiencies indefinitely—if deficits continue to mount year after year." The Dome lost $4 million in its first year of operation, even with its favorable Jazz contract. If new funds couldn't be found, the facility would have to close its doors on April 1.[59]

SSI was a large part of the expense and frustration. But it had also been a boon to the black community in New Orleans, providing thousands of otherwise nonexistent jobs. "It is the embryo of the future for New Orleans," argued Dillard professor Daniel Thompson. "The structure of the corporation itself guarantees black jobs, or at least an integrated enterprise. We must talk about this in the context that in the next four or five years the majority of the population in New Orleans will be black."[60] But still the stadium was broke; still SSI was mired in controversy. "No one is going to make this thing make money unless you convert it into a gambling casino," joked Edwards, "which I do not propose to do." But the governor did have other proposals. The Dome could use funds appropriated to pay state bonds due in June. Ultimately, those bonds would keep the stadium from closing.[61]

SSI remained under fire, and as 1976 became 1977, that fire was also coming from a new direction. Beginning December 31, 1976, a group of SSI employees represented by the Service Employees International Union went on strike at the Dome for better benefits and overtime provisions. And SSI's handling of the strike only led to more racial controversy. "A black wrong is just as bad as a white wrong," said A. Philip Randolph Institute spokesman Carl Galmon, responding to SSI's attempts to undermine union leadership during the picketing. "The actions of SSI administrators is inconsistent with the goals of black people in this city and country." Though the strike didn't last long, such publicity hurt the business's claims that its contract was necessary for race equity in New Orleans. Galmon told reporters that SSI was "pimping the black community." Superdome employees were "making salaries below the national poverty level, while administrators of the organization are making $25,000 a year."[62]

SSI was susceptible to replacement. Hyatt, a reliable national corporation, owned the hotel next door to the Superdome. And it argued as early as August 1976 that it would be the best choice for managing the Dome. In May 1977, Governor Edwards announced that Hyatt would take over all stadium operations. The legislature voiced its approval at the podium and at the ballot.[63] Louisiana's black leaders, however, threatened to boycott the Dome in response to the SSI ouster. "I see it as a $200 million gift to the rich white people with nothing whatsoever coming to the black community but a couple of funky, funky jobs," said attorney Lolis Elie. But Hyatt responded in November 1977 by hiring two African Americans to management positions in the organization.[64] The racial tension abated—for the moment.

Meanwhile, the Jazz, one of the principal entities associated with the Dome and its racial problems, was suffering its own financial difficulties. In response, ownership decided to take its civic case to those with far more resources, turning to a group of investors led by Lee Schlesinger, a third-generation New Orleans real estate mogul. At association meetings in June 1977, the NBA approved Schlesinger's 30 percent minority stake. He had venture capital and did not require an immediate return on his investment. "I consider this a civic endeavor," he explained, acknowledging the financial risk of sinking money into the team.[65]

Van Breda Kolff was fired and replaced by Elgin Baylor during the 1976–77 season. Van Breda Kolff's rigid style clashed with Maravich's improvisation, but he was beloved in the city as, in the words of Mark Kriegel, "everybody's drinking buddy." The hard-drinking coach had earned the devotion of fans, and when he was fired in favor of Baylor, those fans were not happy. "My life was threatened," Mendelson claimed. "I had to have a security guy with me for six months. People were coming up to me at the games and the cops had to step in front of them. The cops thought they were going to shoot me."[66] Even Baylor, however, could not solve team's problems. The Jazz finished with a losing record in the 1976–77 season and in Baylor's subsequent two full years as head coach.[67]

In 1977, the Jazz also hired a new general manager, former agent Lew Schaffel, whose first major move was the acquisition of Atlanta free agent Leonard "Truck" Robinson, one of his principal clients. "They didn't even know the basketball was round," said Hundley of Mendelson and Schaffel, "and they were running the franchise!" Schaffel saw Robinson as the team's future and Maravich as a hindrance to his success. Robinson was thus free to take a thinly veiled shot at Pete and claim that the team "didn't have enough ball movement." In Maravich's words, Schaffel was "a lying back-stabbing son of a bitch who's been out to get me from the start."[68]

The following season, the relationship did not improve when Robinson held out in training camp despite having five years left on his contract. "The Jazz has two sets of rules," said Robinson's agent, "one for Pete and one for the rest of the players." While Robinson eventually reported to camp, there was no way to escape the racial nature of the conflict: the team's outspoken black newcomer was demanding more money and scapegoating the home-state white star. It was a situation not unfamiliar to Maravich and certainly not unnoticed. "I'm the white boy making the most money, so it's my fault." By 1977, there was legitimate criticism of Maravich in the city, as the team's lack of success rankled. But the Great White Hope would always benefit from comparison with a loud, entitled newcomer when race became part of the saga. And race was always part of the New Orleans saga. It was one of the reasons Maravich had been the franchise's first player.[69]

Or Maravich would always benefit from such a comparison in the mainstream white press. The *Louisiana Weekly* had thrilled to the early efforts of the ABA's Buccaneers, emphasizing the team's black players from Louisiana black colleges. The paper focused on Jim Jones and Marlbert Pradd, then on the exploits of Steve Jones. Its coverage of the Jazz, however, would demonstrate far less interest. To be sure, part of that absence of reporting resulted from more comprehensive treatment in the city's white mainstream newspapers. The integration of sports made the black press largely compensatory in the coverage of professionals. The major reason for the paper's unwillingness to devote more resources and page space to the Jazz, however, was the composition of the team. Far from making efforts to recruit players from local black colleges, the team spent the bulk of its resources on Pete Maravich, demonstrating a decidedly different personnel strategy than its predecessor.

In addition to crippling the team to acquire a white star, the Jazz never advertised in the local black newspaper, refusing to court black fans the way its ABA predecessor had. The *Weekly*'s N. R. Davidson did provide a brief weekly update on the Jazz at the outset of the team's run in New Orleans, but he was not overly impressed. The team's first exhibition game in the city drew far fewer fans than the reported two thousand for "a lethargic affair." Time didn't make much of an improvement. "The Jazz is still trying to get it together having dropped its first three league games (what'd you expect)," Davidson reported. "Now we're hearing it again that they're tired. Well at this writing they've got exactly 79 more games to go before they can get a good rest." If that weren't enough, Robertson did not seem interested in giving playing time to the team's draft choice from Grambling. "Folks have been calling in to ask why Aaron James, the Jazz number one draft pick, has not been playing."[70]

Under the leadership of Morton Downey, drafting players from state black colleges had been an effective way to maintain black interest in the team. The Jazz seemed to have been following that model with the choice of James, but its effort would count for naught if he never saw the court. Davidson continued to serve as the designated commentator on Jazz basketball for the early portion of that first season, devoting a small section of his column to the team. With that exception, the *Weekly* remained largely uninterested in the Maravich-led Jazz. The paper only carried sporadic coverage of the club through its rocky tenure in New Orleans.[71]

The racial motivations behind that disinterest were laid bare as the team closed its final unsuccessful season in the city. "I have said it before and I will say it again," wrote the *Weekly*'s Champ Clark. "By and large, there is, perhaps, more racial bias and prejudice emanating from members of the local sports media than anywhere in the nation." He cited the race-baiting of NFL receiver Kenny Burroughs and of boxer Muhammad Ali. Clark noted that racial coverage was present in New Orleans, too. "So, the local writers covering the Jazz games, intimated and implied that most of the Jazz problems would be solved with the trade of Truck Robinson. Prejudice is reflected, too in the makeup of the local TV and radio stations," he argued. "Why isn't some black star on the airways? Neither Channels 4, 6, or 8 have Black Sportscasters on air as anchormen. That is one of the things that Truck meant by Double standards. Look at the stat teams at the games. The only Black you will see is George Wilkes. The Jazz employed several hostesses. Why couldn't one be Black[?] How can these persons assigned to the papers and radio and TV stations accurately report a game when they have been nursed, suckled and weaned on the theory that White is superior and Black is inferior?" Clark celebrated the fact that Robinson's trade to Phoenix put him in the playoffs while the Jazz sat at home after another losing season. It was a statement summed up the root of black disinterest in the Jazz. Unlike the Buccaneers, the Jazz had been largely uninterested in black support and had made no effort to court it.[72]

Thus the team was without finances, victories, a large fan following, and a stadium of its own that could accommodate easy scheduling in January and February. Battistone and his fellow owners began to look elsewhere. Hyatt Management Corporation, which had taken over management of the Superdome from SSI, booked a series of trade shows and conventions during basketball season that dramatically limited possible home dates for the Jazz. Hyatt calculated that profit would simply be higher for such conventions than for a basketball team that averaged a mere four thousand fans in the 1978–79 season. The corporation's decision exacerbated the team's financial losses at a time, five years into the New Orleans NBA experiment, when it was finally supposed to be profitable. And so in April 1979 the Jazz began talks with officials in Salt Lake City, Utah, about the possibility of relocating. Though Salt Lake was an even smaller market than New Orleans, it was more affluent and had a history of success with the ABA's Utah Stars. In addition, Sam Battistone was a devoted member of the Mormon Church.[73]

The Stars had dissipated only three years prior. When the ABA and NBA merged in 1976, four of the upstart teams moved to the more established league, leaving Utah without an organization. Merger discussions between the two leagues had occurred regularly since 1970, when the struggling New Orleans Buccaneers were one of the signposts of ABA difficulty. The team's publicly inflated average attendance had hovered at 2,494 fans per game. While the original merger effort stalled after a group of fourteen NBA players filed an antitrust lawsuit, talks remained ongoing. The Buccaneers' leadership had discussed options in both Kansas City and Salt Lake City before the team moved to Memphis that season. When the New Orleans to Salt Lake ABA move fell through, Utah instead became the home of the former Anaheim Amigos, the team that became the Stars, and stayed in Salt Lake until the merger. The merger was the first substantial league change after the addition of New Orleans. Before the decade was through, the move would compensate Utah with its first NBA franchise.[74]

Regardless, Battistone planned his move without informing Hyatt Management, which responded to the news by reminding the team that it was in its fourth year of a ten-year lease. "We are looking forward to next season," a spokesman said. The Jazz countered by arguing in cryptic language that Hyatt "has breached its agreement" with the team, "and that leaves us free to do what we want to do." When pressed on what exactly the breach entailed, the team refused to comment.[75]

Times-Picayune sports editor Bob Roeseler attempted to call the team's bluff, arguing, "[It] sounds like the Jazz brass is preparing to set up the Superdome as the 'heavy' in this little fairy tale. You know, the big, bad Dome is running the poor little Jazz to Utah." That, he claimed, was a red herring: "The fact of the matter is that the Jazz operation here has been a disaster. Attendance has dwindled to a precious few." To make things worse, the Jazz "have no general manager, they're looking for a new coach, and they've made some bad trades." The Superdome presented scheduling problems, but they were problems eliminated with better management and better play. The *Picayune*'s Jimmy Smith argued that neither Superdome scheduling nor Hyatt Management was the problem. "The failing situation the New Orleans Jazz finds itself in," he wrote, "can be traced to one basic fact—those who know hamburgers don't necessarily know basketball."[76]

Though the *States-Item*'s coverage began by announcing that the Jazz's "love affair with New Orleans has ended," columnist Peter Finney was not convinced. "The most important question," he asked, was "Will NBA owners submit to the wishes of Sam Battistone and allow the Jazz to move to Salt Lake City? The most important answer: They will not." The *Times-Picayune*'s Will Peneguy maintained the theme. "In their infinite chili-burger-to-go wisdom," the team's California ownership had decided to move the team to Salt Lake City after a falling-out with a Chicago-based management company. "Somewhere in the middle of this controversy involving Utah, California, and Illinois, someone has forgotten about the people of New Orleans." It was an understandable frustration. The chamber of commerce responded similarly by urging the team to stay, calling the Jazz "an integral part of the sports culture here."[77]

But the team was not integral to New Orleans's sports culture, and no one had forgotten about the city's people. The Jazz averaged roughly four thousand fans per game in its final season in the cavernous Superdome, and poor attendance drove most professional sports relocation decisions. Still, Ernest Morial, the city's first African American mayor, met with team officials in an effort to convince them to reconsider, but to no avail. Lee Schlesinger and the local minority ownership tried to help by announcing that they would divest themselves of their 30 percent stake in the team should it move to Salt Lake. When attempts to placate Battistone and the California ownership group failed, Morial sent telegrams to every NBA owner reminding them that the fans of New Orleans "are understandably distressed at actions taken by the majority owner of the New Orleans Jazz."

They had "supported the Jazz well during the existence of the team, despite the fact that the Jazz has never reached the playoffs."[78]

In late April, the Salt Lake City Chamber of Commerce announced that it had raised $10,000 in a season-ticket drive to demonstrate to the NBA that Salt Lake was a viable professional city. In May, the team submitted a proposal to the NBA requesting permission to move the Jazz to Utah. Though it was not intended for public consumption, the proposal was leaked to the local press and its arguments ridiculed by local commentators. The document acknowledged that the Jazz had failed to field anything resembling a championship team, and that success on the court could change many of its fortunes, "but it is a fact of life that most NBA teams are not champions—and it would be imprudent to base business survival decisions on the success or lack of success of the basketball team." It was a fairly baffling statement, to be sure.[79]

The Jazz built its argument for relocation on its problems with the Superdome, the "socio-economic makeup of the population," and the city's "current antagonism toward Jazz operations." It was, the team claimed, "very difficult to get fans to regularly attend several games scheduled in short periods of time, especially in New Orleans where a relatively smaller population base and low economic base combine to restrict the draw when home games are spaced too closely together." It was a way of scapegoating the city and the Superdome for the players' broader lack of success. "As has been the case with most of the New Orleans Jazz' managerial decisions," wrote a frustrated Jimmy Smith, the team's relocation proposal "is loaded with errors and ridiculous logic." Such mistakes frustrated those in the media and business community who had acted as boosters for the team.[80]

That month Mayor Morial announced the formation of a "Save Our Jazz Committee," which followed Battistone's and the Jazz management's signing a twenty-year lease with Salt Lake City. The committee's creation was a public-relations move more than a good-faith effort to actually keep the team. But city officials had to save face in the wake of the transfer, and they did legitimately want to maintain the franchise in New Orleans. "Until the news release of three weeks ago," said Morial, "we had no knowledge of any intention to relocate the franchise elsewhere."[81] Louisiana governor Edwin

Edwards supported Morial and the city. "I am not going to allow the state to be blackmailed or blackjacked by owners seeking to feather their nest," he said. Jimmy Smith argued that "it is as if a spouse began divorce proceedings, while the partner was totally unaware of the marital problem that necessitates the break up." In response to the new organization and in an effort to convince the team to stay, a group of protesters in the city collected four thousand signatures on a petition they promised to hand over to the "Save Our Jazz Committee."[82]

At the federal level, Senator Russell Long talked to Larry O'Brien, who had replaced Walter Kennedy as NBA commissioner in 1975, and convinced him to delay a vote on the team's move for at least a week. Long hoped to provide time for a new ownership group led by officials of the Fair Grounds racetrack to buy the team and keep it in New Orleans. Ultimately, the racecourse passed. "We were very enthused," said Fair Grounds president Joseph B. Dorignac, "until we went through all the Jazz's financial statements." He explained that the Jazz had "a lot of deferred payments that ran the thing up much more than it appeared." And even with its disastrous financial situation, Battistone and the ownership group wanted $12.0 million for a team that originally cost $6.1 million prior to all of the failure and debt. "You can't be that civic-minded," said Dorignac, "to dig down into your pockets all the way down to your ankles."[83]

The failure of the Fair Grounds bid, however, would not be the end of the Jazz saga, as the city became far more interested in the team after its planned move. Hyatt Management threatened a lawsuit that would include the city, state, radio, and television distributors, among others, as plaintiffs. "We will sue the (Jazz) owners, the league and every member of the league," promised Hyatt president Denzil Skinner.[84] The Hyatt lawsuit did go forward, and in July a New Orleans civil-court judge issued a ten-day restraining order halting the Jazz from moving to Salt Lake City. However, the $7.0 million bond the judge required of Hyatt for the order was prohibitive. The NBA wanted the bond because delay carried with it the possibility of a heavy financial burden on the league, which was then finalizing the coming season's schedule. And while the high bond kept Hyatt from paying and prevented the restraining order from holding the team in New Orleans, the city added pressure to the Jazz by joining the suit. New Orleans asked the team for an additional $17.9 million, $10.0 million for "damage to its good will and reputation," and another $7.9 million for "loss of revenue" the moved caused. The city claimed that the team owed an additional $24,000 in amusement taxes and $14,000 in sales taxes.[85]

Meanwhile, the *Times-Picayune*'s Jimmy Smith reveled in the fact that Battistone's Sambo's chain was falling on hard times. The business's income fell from $22.8 million in 1977 to $7.6 million the following year. At an annual stockholders' meeting, "shareholders charged that the restaurant chain's declining profit during the last 18 months reflected poor management, that Sambo's 1,060 restaurants were too often badly run." Smith was delighted. "It seems that the Jazz isn't the only business that Sam Battistone is running into problems with." If the team moved to Salt Lake City, wrote journalist James Haddican, "the name would have to be changed to something more appropriate like the Saltines or the Choirboys." And "if they play there the way they played here, the lot of them could turn into pillars of salt."[86]

Ultimately, the NBA's owners voted unanimously to approve the team's move to Utah, basing their decision in particular "in terms of low season ticket sales and poor playing dates." By the time of the team's exodus to Salt Lake City, the Jazz was running at a $5 million dollar deficit. After the vote, Morial tried and failed to refute the owners' explanation. The decision "should be a warning to other cities," he lamented. "No matter how well a city supports its professional teams, a franchise can be moved at the whim of an owner."[87] Jimmy Smith wrote, "There will be no more bows, no more encores, no more opening nights. The final curtain rang down on the New Orleans Jazz." The team announced that it would reimburse the "several hundred holders of minority interests in the Jazz" who had purchased shares during the first season. While these shares were meant to alleviate the team's early debt, that debt was never relieved.[88]

In mid-July, however, a judge in civil district court approved the city and state's request for an injunction against the team's move. As governmental entities they were not required to provide the same bond as Hyatt, and thus the stay order went through. State attorney general William Guste announced later that month that he would seek a contempt of court citation against the

Jazz for violating the new order prohibiting the move to Utah. The citation was dismissed for lack of evidence. Meanwhile, testimony in the Hyatt lawsuit commenced in Orleans Parish Civil District Court. The D. H. Holmes Company, ticket broker for the team in New Orleans, also filed suit against the Jazz, seeking $1.3 million in damages for breach of contract.[89]

Ultimately, however, the suits were unsuccessful, the civil district court denying in early August the city and state's injunction request and opening the way for the team's move to Salt Lake City. An eleventh-hour effort by the state and by Hyatt to file in the Fourth Circuit Court of Appeals failed to keep the Jazz in place, the appeals court arguing that the suit lacked "sufficient cause or legal basis." The appellate court did, however, rule that state antitrust laws applied to the team. Thus Hyatt and its co-plaintiffs could seek damages.[90]

As the team packed up and began its move west, Battistone's restaurant began encountering a series of lawsuits over its name. The NAACP, National Urban League, and several human rights commissions were involved in many of the proceedings. During the Jazz's first Utah season, six hundred Sambo's managers struck in response to corporate restructuring. More lawsuits followed, as well as health code violations. In 1982, the chain filed for bankruptcy, completing an ignominious decline that began around the same time that New Orleans professional basketball was experiencing its own.[91]

The Jazz's end resulted from several intervening factors: the racial stigma attendant on professional basketball and the management of the Superdome; the failure of the team to win, largely because of mismanagement and the leveraging of future draft picks to acquire Pete Maravich; and an absentee management that left an organizational vacuum in New Orleans. Mostly, however, the team failed because the Deep South city attempted to take its place in the post–civil rights era Sunbelt by adding professional sports that it simply was not ready to accommodate. In that sense, the Jazz's problems were the same intertwined southern issues the Buccaneers and the Hawks faced—the unlearned lessons of the ghosts of basketball past.

CONCLUSION

As the Jazz were absconding from New Orleans, off to Salt Lake City for a fresh start outside of the Deep South, Dominique Wilkins, a three-time high school champion and a McDonald's All-American from Washington, North Carolina, began his freshman year at the University of Georgia. He came to Athens as the most heralded basketball recruit in the school's history. It was a confluence of events that signaled that even as New Orleans lost its NBA team, the foundation for the Deep South's acceptance of the game, and thus the association's eventual return to New Orleans, was being laid on the University of Georgia campus. Wilkins dominated the SEC much as he had dominated North Carolina high school basketball, and in 1981 he was named conference player of the year. After his junior season at Georgia, Wilkins entered the NBA draft. He was selected third overall by the team that had moved at the same time he had moved three years earlier—the Jazz, now based in Utah.[1]

Wilkins, however, knew the troubled history of the Jazz in New Orleans and was reluctant to sign with the team. Meanwhile, the Jazz had yet to emerge from the financial hole it had begun digging in New Orleans; it desperately needed liquid capital. Thus it was that, several months after the draft, the former Deep South team traded with the only remaining Deep South team. The Jazz sent Wilkins to the Atlanta Hawks in exchange for John Drew, Freeman Williams, and $1 million in cash. Though Wilkins would not lead the Hawks to a championship in the 1980s or 1990s, he would lead them to a new prominence. As a nine-time all-star and an association scoring champion, he helped the Hawks achieve five consecutive fifty-win seasons. That combination of legitimate success, entertaining basketball, and a black player whom the fans embraced as a local from the University of Georgia spurred professional basketball's first legitimate success in the Deep South.[2]

The rise of Wilkins and the new acceptance of the Hawks did not happen in a vacuum. In the 1970s, Atlanta elected a black mayor, Maynard Holbrook Jackson, the first black leader in a Deep South metropolitan area. His election was controversial, as his opponent, incumbent Sam Massell, in the words of historian Alton Hornsby, "hinted that the city would die under black leadership." But the city did not die. Jackson served two terms and ushered in an age of black leadership in Atlanta. With Jackson as mayor, the city was becoming known as the "black Mecca of the South," according to an *Ebony* magazine profile, a city that offered "the possibility of peaceful—and profitable—racial coexistence." City boosters noted biracial cooperation in civic and business partnerships and a growing number of black business-people moving to Atlanta for work. Still, most black businesses were relatively small, and more than two-thirds of city residents living below the poverty line were black.[3]

Andrew Jackson Young succeeded Jackson and served as mayor for most of the 1980s. Though Young sought to build his record on fighting crime, he was largely unsuccessful. A crisis in the levels of violent crime and the illicit drug trade during Young's tenure put Atlanta, according to Hornsby, "at or near the top of all major American cities, particularly in violent crimes." The city had "the second-highest poverty rate in the nation" in the 1980s, "a large homeless population, and a high—but declining—high school drop-out rate." Still, white civic leaders became accustomed to the demographic changes in the city that virtually assured black leadership would continue. Suburban white flight that made residents inside the Atlanta city limits majority black immediately facilitated this leadership. Civic leaders' familiarity with these changes slowly turned into begrudging acceptance.[4]

That acceptance would also reach the Hawks, pushed by that broader "coexistence" and Wilkins and the team's success. That success, however, was also significant as a result of another civic imperative: Atlanta's other professional teams weren't good. While the Atlanta Braves managed to win eighty-nine games in 1982 and reach the National League Championship Series, it would be the team's last postseason appearance until 1991. With the exception of 1983, it would be the team's last winning season that decade. The NFL's Falcons won five games and lost four in a strike-shortened 1982 season, but the team never managed a winning season through the rest of the decade. Its next playoff appearance came in 1991, the same year as its baseball counterpart. Meanwhile, from 1985 to 1989, the Wilkins-led Hawks won at least fifty games per season in spectacular fashion, with a high-potency offense that emphasized fast breaks and slam dunks.[5] Thus the city beset by crime and poverty, coming to terms with new leadership, turned to its predominantly black NBA team as a symbol of success and racial progress.

"Had Sir Isaac Newton seen Dominique Wilkins," wrote the *Houston Chronicle*'s Alan Truex in 1986, "the law of gravity might never have been written."[6] And so the team signed him that year to a new five-year, $6.3 million contract, a "contract that secures the Hawks' future for the next five years," Hawks' general manager Stan Kasten announced proudly. "It will provide Dominique with lifetime security."[7] Wilkins was powerful, but humble. He was black, but he was also compatible with white assumptions about black athletes. "I'd spend my last twenty dollars," Wilkins would say years after his playing days, while working in the Hawks' front office, "at Stone Mountain Park with my son."[8]

Such is not to say that Wilkins encountered no difficulties during his time in Atlanta. The team never won a championship, for example. Also, in April 1989, at the end of the Hawks' final fifty-win season of the decade, reporters discovered that Wilkins had taken $30,000 from an agent while a student at the University of Georgia.[9] That year, after another successful season and another failure to win a championship, the *Atlanta Constitution*'s

Dave Kindred even called for Wilkins to be traded, assuming that the team's ceiling with the athlete had been reached. Kindred was right, though the Human Highlight Film would stay in Atlanta until being traded to the Los Angeles Clippers in 1994. By that time, however, the Hawks were an accepted part of the fabric of the city.[10]

Such is also not to say that Wilkins acted alone. He was joined by star black players like Doc Rivers, Kevin Willis, Tree Rollins, Antoine Carr, Spud Webb, and, beginning in 1988, Moses Malone, all of whom contributed to the team's successful run and thus endeared themselves to the city. And they endeared themselves to the black residents of the city. Fans thrilled to the highlights of Wilkins and his teammates. The *Atlanta Daily World* covered the team in detail throughout the run of 1980s success, but the paper also emphasized the racial trailblazing at work. For example, when Hawks coach Mike Fratello hosted his December 1988 holiday party at a local country club that did not offer memberships to black customers, Wilkins, Rivers, and Reggie Theus refused to attend. "Believe it or not," wrote the *World*'s Chico Renfro, "there are still some professional athletes that are strong enough to speak out against racism."[11]

Scheduled at an all-too-commonly restricted club, Fratello's party demonstrated that the Atlanta of the 1980s was still, decades after the Civil Rights Act of 1964, a predominantly segregated city. "Highways, the displacement of blacks, the manipulation of public housing site selection and other similar tactics," Ronald Bayor explains, played a decided role in the 1970s and 1980s in developing a dramatically segregated city.[12] Or, in the words of historian Kevin Kruse, "By the end of the 1960s, the effects of white resistance to desegregation and white flight from it were apparent to all Atlantans." During the following decade, and as a result of white flight out of the city that had been developing since the birth of the civil rights movement, "suburbanites severed all local ties with the city."[13]

Such problems still have not abandoned Deep South metropolises like Atlanta. When the Hawks' home arena, the Omni, was demolished in 1997, its replacement, Philips Arena, was built on the same property. The team remains downtown in the second decade of the twenty-first century. Yet the Braves have taken a different tack. In constructing their new stadium in northern suburban Cobb County, the team moved from a predominantly black area to a predominantly white, middle- and upper-class area. The location is difficult for the city's poor black residents to access, but it is easy to reach for those suburban residents who inherited the postwar white flight that ultimately generated Atlanta's demographic shift. Many have interpreted the new Braves stadium, Suntrust Park, as an antagonistic act toward the city's black residents. The structure demonstrates that the pitfalls of race and sport have not fully ceased in the Deep South.

The Hawks, too, have had their own racial issues. While the Braves were in the process of building Suntrust Park, the Hawks' general manager, Danny Ferry, was forced to resign after making racial remarks about a potential player in 2014. In 2015, then-owner Bruce Levenson sent an email to employees complaining that the Hawks' "overwhelmingly black" fan base was "scaring away whites." Levenson eventually sold the team in response to the resulting scandal, and the team ultimately hired a chief diversity and inclusion officer to regulate its racial policies and racial publicity. In July 2017, as the Braves were playing their first season in their new Cobb County stadium, the Hawks faced a racial discrimination lawsuit by a former manager of security operations. The manager claimed that white celebrities were given preferential treatment by the team, while black celebrities were not, and that he was fired for complaining about the discrepancy.[14]

The Wilkins-led Hawks won a franchise record fifty-seven games in 1987. The following season, Charlotte, North Carolina, was awarded an expansion NBA franchise. Though the city was not in the Deep South, its new team, the Hornets, demonstrated that interest in the sport was growing in the broader region. In 1989, the last of the Hawks' consecutive fifty-win seasons, the NBA awarded another expansion franchise to Orlando, a city just south of Sanford, Florida, where Jackie Robinson had been chased away from Dodgers spring training forty-three years prior. Times had decidedly changed.[15]

While Wilkins was the lynchpin of the white South's modern turn to acceptance of professional basketball, the Buccaneers, Hawks, and Jazz were the foundation upon which the turn took place. The change was fully realized in the early twenty-first century. In 2001, with a diminishing fan presence in both Charlotte and Vancouver, both NBA franchises petitioned the association to move to Memphis, Tennessee. Vancouver ultimately won this contest; however, the acrimony in Charlotte had not abated. Fans blamed the owner for a lack of success, and the owner blamed Charlotte for a crumbling arena. In 2002, this fight led to the team's move to New Orleans, giving the city an NBA franchise for the first time since the departure of the Jazz in 1979. The transition to a legitimate professional basketball culture in the Deep South was complete.[16]

In October 2002, the Jazz returned to New Orleans for the first time since its hasty departure in 1979, taking on the city's new NBA team, the Hornets, in the franchise's first official game in its new location. Former New Orleans Jazz players attended, and the new New Orleans team retired Maravich's jersey.[17] It would take longer for the Hawks to do the same. Despite Maravich's important legacy in Atlanta, its attendant baggage would keep the team from giving him the same honor. The Hawks finally retired his jersey in March 2017, sixteen seasons after the franchise had done the same for Wilkins. The month following the Jazz's first return to its original home in 2002, the Hornets played the Hawks twice in a brief two-week span. One game was held in New Orleans, the other in Atlanta, with each team winning on its home floor. The games were not sold out, but the crowds were large and lively—17,128 attended in Atlanta, and 15,259 attended in New Orleans. There was no particular fanfare, as they were just two more games on the schedule. Professional basketball was no longer an anomaly in the Deep South. It had finally arrived.[18]

NOTES

· ·

INTRODUCTION

1. Gary Davidson, *Breaking the Game Wide Open* (New York: Atheneum, 1974), 31; and Bob Ryan, *The Pro Game: The World of Professional Basketball* (New York: McGraw-Hill, 1975), 11–13.

2. Bob Ryan, *Pro Game*, 17. For more on the development of professional basketball and the role of the black player in that development, see Oceania Chalk, *Pioneers of Black Sport: The Early Days of the Black Professional Athlete in Baseball, Basketball, Boxing, and Football* (New York: Dodd, Mead, 1975), 83–120.

3. James W. Silver, *Mississippi: The Closed Society* (1964; repr., Jackson: University Press of Mississippi, 2012), 6.

4. While there is no specific causal chain connecting the events, it seems relevant to note that Sanford would earn infamy again in 2012 as the site of the killing of Trayvon Martin. For more on Robinson, see Thomas Aiello, "The Robinson Interregnum: The Black Press Responds to the Signing of Jackie Robinson, October 23, 1945–March 1, 1946," *Readex Report* 12 (March 2017), www.readex.com. While there are myriad works on Robinson, the most comprehensive treatment of his life is Arnold Rampersad, *Jackie Robinson: A Biography* (New York: Random House, 1997).

5. As the Royals moved to Cincinnati, so too did the Fort Wayne Pistons move to Detroit. In 1963, the Syracuse Nationals moved to Philadelphia, permanently eliminating small markets from the NBA. Steven A. Riess, *City Games: The Evolution of*

American Urban Society and the Rise of Sports (Urbana: University of Illinois Press, 1991), 232–33.

6. David George Surdam, *The Rise of the National Basketball Association* (Urbana: University of Illinois Press, 2012), 83, 164, 168.

CHAPTER 1

1. Goldberg was also known for signing five black players for his White Huts team in 1942. The move was less an intentional statement of equality and more an attempt to offset wartime draft absences, but it made the White Huts one of the first integrated professional teams in American sports. *Toledo Blade*, February 12, 2017, D1; Bill Russell, *Go Up for Glory* (New York: Coward-McCann, 1966), 113–15, 116–17, 118–19; Jeffrey Denberg, Roland Lazenby, and Tom Stinson, *From Sweet Lou to 'Nique* (Atlanta: Longstreet, 1992), 31; Chet Walker, "On the Road in the South, 1960," in *The Unlevel Playing Field: A Documentary History of the African American Experience in Sport*, ed. David K. Wiggins and Patrick B. Miller (Urbana: University of Illinois Press, 2005), 277–82; and Jeff Marcus, *A Biographical Dictionary of Professional Basketball Coaches* (Lanham, MD: Scarecrow, 2003), 140.

2. *Times-Picayune* (New Orleans), November 14, 1947, 23; Murray R. Nelson, *The National Basketball League: A History, 1935–1949* (Jefferson, NC: McFarland, 2009), 179–80, 211; and John Grasso, *Historical Dictionary of Basketball* (Lanham, MD: Scarecrow, 2011), 300.

3. Nelson, *The National Basketball League*, 179–80, 211; Grasso, *Historical Dictionary of Basketball*, 300; Marcus, *Biographical Dictionary of Professional Basketball Coaches*, 140; Eric M. Leifer, *Making the Majors: The Transformation of Team Sports in America* (Cambridge, MA: Harvard University Press, 1995), 112–17; *New York Times*, November 14, 1947, 32; and *Washington Post*, September 5, 1947, B8, November 14, 1947, B4.

4. Pailet, a leading Jewish figure in New Orleans, was also involved in other sports work in the city. He was, for example, a charter member of the New Orleans Mid-Winter Sports Association, which sponsored the annual Sugar Bowl. *Town Talk* (Alexandria, LA), June 11, 1978, 3; Marcus, *Biographical Dictionary of Professional Basketball Coaches*, 301; and *Times-Picayune* (New Orleans), October 12, 1947, 5-5, October 30, 1947, 22.

5. *Times-Picayune* (New Orleans), November 9, 1947, 3, November 10, 1947, 21, 22, November 11, 1947, 14, 15.

6. The team finished with a 3-5 record, ranking second from the bottom of the league's Southern Division. *Times-Picayune* (New Orleans), November 12, 1947, 21, November 14, 1947, 23; Mary Lou Widmer, *New Orleans in the Thirties* (Gretna, LA: Pelican, 1989), 130–32; Federal Writer's Project of the Works Progress Administration, *New Orleans City Guide, 1938* (1938; repr., New Orleans: Garret County Press, 2011), xxxix, xl; and Roger Meyer, "Professional Basketball League of America, 1947–48," Association for Professional Basketball Research website, accessed June 20, 2016, www.apbr.org/pbla.html.

7. *Atlanta Constitution*, October 31, 1947, 14.

8. Ibid., October 12, 1947, 16C, November 14, 1947, 8.

9. Ibid., November 4, 1947, 18; and *New York Times*, September 12, 1947, 29.

10. *Atlanta Constitution*, November 12, 1947, 13.

11. Ibid., November 5, 1947, 10.

12. Ibid., November 13, 1947, 18.

13. League executive Harry Foote claimed in the wake of Brooks's announcement that he "couldn't add any more to the statement except that the league had been disbanded." *Christian Science Monitor*, November 13, 1947, 14; and *New York Herald Tribune*, November 14, 1947, 29.

14. The National Basketball League voted to allow players' return in early December, giving athletes like Rader an escape route back to their original teams. *Atlanta Constitution*, November 14, 1947, 8, December 4, 1947, 14; and *Chicago Tribune*, December 5, 1947, 52.

15. *Times-Picayune* (New Orleans), September 3, 1947, 25, October 10, 1947, 27; *Atlanta Constitution*, October 7, 1947, 20; "Raymond Johnson," *Editor and Publisher* 81 (1948): 40; Bill Traughber, *Nashville Sports History: Stories from the Stands* (Charleston: History Press, 2010), 111–14; and Jack Black, Robert Bradley, and Al Kirk, "History of the Southern Basketball League," Association for Professional Basketball Research website, accessed June 20, 2016, www.apbr.org/sbl4749.html.

16. *Nashville Tennessean*, September 2, 1947, 22, September 3, 1947, 16, 17, September 4, 1947, 20, September 9, 1947, 14.

17. *Atlanta Constitution*, September 3, 1947, 18.

18. *Nashville Tennessean*, December 4, 1947, 26, 27, December 9, 1947, 28.

19. Ibid., March 3, 1948, 16, March 7, 1948, 32, March 8, 1948, 13, March 9, 1948, 16, 17, March 10, 1948, 16, 17, March 11, 1948, 14, 15, March 12, 1948, 51, March 13, 1948, 7, March 14, 1948, 1B, 2B, March 15, 1948, 10.

20. *Times-Picayune* (New Orleans), November 23, 1948, 26; and Black, Bradley, and Kirk, "History of the Southern Basketball League."

21. *Times-Picayune* (New Orleans), November 29, 1948, 26.

22. Ibid., December 1, 1948, 37, December 2, 1948, 21, December 7, 1948, 23.

23. The Cover Girls' star was Dot Whalen, who made her name with the All-American Girls Professional Baseball League and was later depicted in the movie *A League of Their Own*. Ibid., January 28, 1949, 21, February 11, 1949, 23, February 13, 1949, 29, February 14, 1949, 36.

24. St. Aloysius would close after the 1969 school year, combining with Gentilly's Cor Jesu High School to create Brother Martin High School the following year. Brother Martin still remains, but not in that location. Ibid., February 17, 1949, 16, January 30, 1949, 29, February 19, 1949, 11, February 20, 1949, 27; and Black, Bradley, and Kirk, "History of the Southern Basketball League."

25. *Chicago Defender*, November 7, 1956, 24.

26. Ibid., February 23, 1959, 24; and Kurt Edward Kemper, *College Football and American Culture in the Cold War Era* (Urbana: University of Illinois Press, 2009), 80–115. Quote from 85. For more on the Sugar Bowl and its struggle with integration, see Lane Demas, *Integrating the Gridiron: Black Civil Rights and American College Football* (New Brunswick, NJ: Rutgers University Press, 2011), 73–101.

27. *Pittsburgh Courier*, February 13, 1960, 19. While the ban on segregated competition fell, the law's prohibition of integrated seating at those contests lasted until 1963.

28. Ibid., March 21, 1953, 26.

29. *Chicago Defender*, February 6, 1954, 24. For more on the integration of southern baseball, see Bruce Adelson, *Brushing Back Jim Crow: The Integration of Minor League Baseball In the American South* (Charlottesville: University of Virginia Press, 2007).

30. *Atlanta Daily World*, June 4, 1954, 7.

31. The teams had been making tours through the South for several years, including similarly contested stops in Atlanta. Ibid., January 17, 1957, 1, December 16, 1955, 7.

32. *Pittsburgh Courier*, February 9, 1957, A6.

33. *Atlanta Daily World*, January 21, 1958, 5.

34. *Baltimore Afro-American*, February 4, 1961, 6.

35. Ibid., May 26, 1962, 9; and *Atlanta Daily World*, May 13, 1962, A5. Such problems also left collegiate athletic conferences like the Southeastern and Southwestern in a state of crisis. Some schools in the Upper South were ready and willing to desegregate athletics teams, and schools in the Deep South were staunchly opposed. *Atlanta Daily World*, May 19, 1962, 24.

36. *Atlanta Daily World*, January 28, 1947, 5, April 9, 1947, 5, October 29, 1947, 5, January 1, 1949, 5. See also John Schleppi, *Chicago's Showcase of Basketball: The World Tournament of Professional Basketball and the College All-Star Game* (Haworth, NJ: St. Johann, 2008).

37. *Atlanta Daily World*, January 28, 1947, 5, April 9, 1947, 5, October 29, 1947, 5, January 1, 1949, 5.

38. The "Swish! Two Points!!" column was penned by the pseudonym "Dribble." For examples of that column and further *Weekly* basketball coverage in the decade, see *Louisiana Weekly*, March 24, 1945, 8, March 31, 1945, 8, February 9, 1946, 6, March 30, 1946, 6.

39. *Atlanta Daily World*, January 13, 1948, 5.

40. Damion L. Thomas, *Globetrotting: African American Athletes and Cold War Politics* (Urbana: University of Illinois Press, 2012), 41–74. Quotes from 43.

41. *Pittsburgh Courier*, January 17, 1953, 25.

42. *Atlanta Daily World*, February 8, 1959, 8; and *Los Angeles Sentinel*, January 22, 1959, A6.

43. *Atlanta Daily World*, February 8, 1959, 8; *Los Angeles Sentinel*, January 22, 1959, A6; and Bijan C. Bayne, *Elgin Baylor: The Man Who Changed Basketball* (Lanham, MD: Rowman and Littlefield, 2015), 43–46.

44. *Los Angeles Sentinel*, January 22, 1959, B5; and *Chicago Defender*, January 21, 1959, 22.

45. *Pittsburgh Courier*, January 24, 1959, 20.

46. *Chicago Defender*, December 2, 1958, A22, December 6, 1958, 12, 23; *Baltimore Afro-American*, December 6, 1958, 1; and *Pittsburgh Courier*, December 6, 1958, A3, January 24, 1959, 20.

47. *Pittsburgh Courier*, February 7, 1959, 21.

48. *Los Angeles Sentinel*, November 12, 1964, B2.

49. *PIttsburgh Courier*, May 12, 1962, A30.

50. Russell, *Go Up for Glory*, 113–15.

51. The players refused services were Bill Russell, K. C. Jones, Tom Sanders, Sam Jones, Al Butler, Woody Sauldsberry, and Cleo Hill. *New York Times*, October 18, 1961, 59.

52. *Pittsburgh Courier*, January 12, 1963, 17. For more on restrictions for black athletes playing in the South, see Oscar Robertson, *The Big O: My Life, My Times, My Game* (New York: Rodale, 2003), 33, 50–55, 99–100, 164–65.

53. Russell, *Go Up for Glory*, 113–15, 116–17, 118–19; Denberg, Lazenby, and Stinson, *From Sweet Lou to 'Nique*, 31; and Walker, "On the Road in the South, 1960," 277–82.

54. Murray R. Nelson, *Abe Saperstein and the American Basketball League, 1960– 1963* (Jefferson, NC: McFarland, 2013), 2–11; and Davidson, *Breaking the Game Wide Open*, 34.

55. *Pittsburgh Courier*, August 17, 1963, C10.

56. *Baltimore Afro-American*, August 17, 1963, 20.

57. Kennedy expected "growth and prosperity" for the league, including team expansion, under his new authoritarian regime. He was also responding to the diminished reputation of college basketball after a series of postwar gambling scandals damaged the game. For example, when Seattle University had a point-shaving scandal two years later, in 1965, All-American Charlie Williams was banned from the NBA. He had to opt for the ABA instead. *Christian Science Monitor*, August 23, 1963, 7, October 23, 1963, 11, December 18, 1963, 12; and Albert J. Figone, *Cheating the Spread: Gamblers, Point Shavers, and Game Fixers in College Football and Basketball* (Urbana: University of Illinois Press, 2012), 111–12. For more on Kennedy's early trenchant moves, see *Christian Science Monitor*, December 11, 1963, 13; and *Washington Post*, November 14, 1963, B3. The planned television transition did occur. The month following the Board of Governors meetings, the NBA released a schedule of eleven televised games for January, February, and March 1964. *Baltimore Afro-American*, September 14, 1963, 7.

58. *Christian Science Monitor*, August 23, 1963, 7, December 18, 1963, 12. For examples of player skepticism over the racial moves of the NBA, see Joe Caldwell, *Banned From Basketball: The Long Strange Trip of "Pogo" Joe Caldwell* (Tempe:

self-pub., 2003); and John Devaney, "Pro Basketball's Hidden Fear," *Sport*, February 1966, 32–33, 89–92. The NBA has a policy of not releasing the minutes of Board of Governors meetings, and it stated that policy in response to the author's requests for access. The 1963 Board of Governors included Ben Kerner of the St. Louis Hawks, Walter A. Brown of the Boston Celtics, Fred Zollner of the Detroit Pistons (formerly of Ft. Wayne), Franklin Mieuli of the San Francisco Warriors, Robert E. Short of the Los Angeles Lakers, Edward S. "Ned" Irish of the New York Knicks, either John Egan or Isaac "Ike" Richman of the Philadelphia 76ers, either Tom Grace or Louis M. Jacobs of the Cincinnati Royals, and Dave Trager of the Baltimore Bullets. None of those executives, however, have archived papers that include copies of such records. That being the case, reports of the NBA's intentions in relation to roster expansion must necessarily be circumstantial. Names of board members compiled from the research of Robert D. Bradley, founder of the Association for Professional Basketball Research. See "Chairman of the Board of Governors/Board of Governors," Association for Professional Basketball Research website, accessed April 1, 2017, www.apbr.org.

59. "As despicable as it was, however," Russell continued, "I must say that the quota system won a title for the Celtics. In the 1963–64 season Cincinnati had a better team than we did. The Royals could have beaten us, but in my opinion they virtually gave Bob Boozer away to get down to their black quota, and that gave us a championship in the bargain." Bill Russell, "Success Is A Journey," *Sports Illustrated*, June 8, 1970, 80–93; and Pete Axthelm, *The City Game: Basketball from the Garden to the Playgrounds* (1970; repr., Lincoln: University of Nebraska Press, 1999), 127. For more on how a similar phenomenon played out in the 1990s, as black antagonism combined with corporate sponsorship culture to differentiate blackness in professional basketball, see Todd Boyd, "The Day the Niggaz Took Over: Basketball, Commodity Culture, and Black Masculinity," in *Out of Bounds: Sports, Media, and the Politics of Identity*, ed. Aaron Baker and Todd Boyd (Bloomington: Indiana University Press, 1997), 123–43.

60. Bayne, *Elgin Baylor*, 128; and *Baltimore Afro-American*, August 17, 1963, 20.

61. *Christian Science Monitor*, December 6, 1963, 11; and Devaney, "Pro Basketball's Hidden Fear," 89.

62. *Washington Post*, April 22, 1963, A25.

63. Devaney, "Pro Basketball's Hidden Fear," 33.

64. Ibid.

65. Ibid., 89.

66. Ibid., 89, 90.

67. Ibid., 90.

68. Ibid.

69. Ibid., 91.

70. Ibid., 90.

71. "The Hidden Fear that Is Not Our Fear," *Sport*, May 1966, 104.

72. Terry Pluto, *Loose Balls: The Short, Wild Life of the American Basketball Association* (New York: Simon and Schuster, 1990), 3–4.

73. Ibid., 69, 77, 90.

CHAPTER 2

1. *Times-Picayune* (New Orleans), June 21, 1967, 1-11.

2. Morton Downey Jr. and William Hoffer, *Mort! Mort! Mort! No Place to Hide* (New York: Delacorte Press), 75–76; Richard Zoglin and William Tynan, "The Pit Bull of Talk-Show Host Morton Downey Jr. Tells Off His Guests—And His Audience," *Time*, January 4, 1988, 76; and Wolfgang Saxon, "Morton Downey Jr., 67, Combative TV Host," *New York Times*, March 14, 2001, B9.

3. Downey and Hoffer, *Mort! Mort! Mort!*, 76–77, 115.

4. *Times-Picayune* (New Orleans), April 12, 1966, 3-10; and ibid., 137.

5. *Times-Picayune* (New Orleans), April 12, 1966, 3-10, January 9, 1967, 2-9.

6. *Times-Picayune* (New Orleans), January 8, 1967, 1-1; and *States-Item* (New Orleans), January 9, 1967, 28. *States-Item* columnist George Sweeney remained skeptical, wondering if the Hawks could "make it at the turnstiles." January 10, 1967, 27. "Plans are afoot by Mort Downey, Jr., to secure a National Basketball League franchise," wrote the *Louisiana Weekly*'s Jim Hall. In Hall's estimation, the city was well on its way to becoming "the No. 1 sports city in the south." *Louisiana Weekly*, January 7, 1967, 14.

7. *States-Item* (New Orleans), January 13, 1967, 14, January 14, 1967, 10, January 17, 1967, 23, February 1, 1967, 18; *Times-Picayune* (New Orleans), January 8, 1967, 1-1, September 6, 1967, 1-1; and *Post-Dispatch* (St. Louis), January 9, 1967, 4C, January 10, 1967, 1A.

8. Louis Ivon to Jim Garrison, Memorandum, September 6, 1967, Statement of Jules Ricco Kimble, Parish of Orleans, Office of the District Attorney, October 10, 1967, Harold Weisberg Archive, Hood College, Frederick, MD; William W. Turner, "The Garrison Commission," *Ramparts Magazine*, January 1968, 68–69; *Times-Picayune* (New Orleans), October 12, 1967, 1-1, October 13, 1967, 1-3, October 17, 1967, 1-15; Gerald Posner, *Killing the Dream: James Earl Ray and the Assassination of Martin Luther King, Jr.* (New York: Random House, 1998), 269–70; and United States v. Clayton Kimble and Jules Ron Kimbel, 719 F.2d 1253 (1983).

9. Loyola University *Maroon*, March 10, 1967, 12; and *Times-Picayune* (New Orleans), January 9, 1967, 2-9.

10. *Times-Picayune* (New Orleans), January 11, 1967, 2-8, January 12, 1967, 2-13.

11. Ibid., January 13, 1967, 2-3, January 14, 1967, 2-4, January 15, 1967, 6-2.

12. Davidson, *Breaking the Game Wide Open*, 36–38; *Times-Picayune* (New Orleans), January 20, 1967, 2-5, January 25, 1967, 2-4, February 4, 1967, 2-4; and *States-Item* (New Orleans), February 3, 1967, 42, February 4, 1967, 10.

13. Pluto, *Loose Balls*, 33, 39–44; Davidson, *Breaking the Game Wide Open*, 27, 34–43; *Atlanta Constitution*, January 22, 1967, 55, February 3, 1967, 31; "Year Round Hockey?" *SportsLetter* 5 (August 1993): 3; *New York Times*, February 3, 1967, 22; and *Christian Science Monitor*, February 4, 1967, 10.

14. *Times-Picayune* (New Orleans), February 1, 1967, 18; James Whiteside, *Colorado: A Sports History* (Niwot: University Press of Colorado, 1999), 315, 317; and Tom Dyja, "History of the NBA," in *Professional Sports Team Histories: Basketball*, ed. Michael L. LaBlanc (Detroit: Gale Research, 1994), 17.

15. Michael Novak, *The Joy of Sports: End Zones, Bases, Baskets, Balls, and the Consecration of the American Spirit* (New York: Basic Books, 1976), 101, 105. Several strong works deal successfully with the blackness of professional basketball, and some of them will be cited throughout this chapter and book. For examples of such studies, see Boyd, "Day the Niggaz Took Over," 134–37; Axthelm, *City Game*; Nelson George, *Elevating the Game: Black Men and Basketball* (New York: HarperCollins, 1992); John Feinstein, *The Punch: One Night, Two Lives, and the Fight that Changed Basketball Forever* (New York: Back Bay Books, 2003); and Jeffrey Lane, *Under the Boards: The Cultural Revolution in Basketball* (Lincoln: University of Nebraska Press, 2007). For examples of studies that include professional basketball in a broader examination of race and sports, see John Hoberman,

Darwin's Athletes: How Sport Has Damaged Black America and Preserved the Myth of Race (New York: Mariner Books, 1997); Kenneth L. Shropshire, *In Black and White: Race and Sports in America* (New York: New York University Press, 1998); William C. Rhoden, *Forty Million Dollar Slaves: The Rise, Fall, and Redemption of the Black Athlete* (New York: Broadway, 2007); Dave Zirin, *What's My Name, Fool? Sports and Resistance in the United States* (Chicago: Haymarket Books, 2005); and Jeffrey T. Sammons, "'Race' and Sport: A Critical, Historical Examination," *Journal of Sport History* 21 (Fall 1994): 203–78.

16. Riess, *City Games*, 107–8. Quote from 107.

17. Ibid., 116–17; Axthelm, *City Game*, ix–x; and Jeffrey T. Sammons, "'Race' and Sport," 243–44.

18. Smith is careful to note that though such teams were integrated, which did potent symbolic work, the black experience at schools like UCLA was still difficult, as players experienced discrimination in student housing, Greek life, and other areas of collegiate life. John Matthew Smith, *The Sons of Westwood: John Wooden, UCLA, and the Dynasty that Changed College Basketball* (Urbana: University of Illinois Press, 2013), 20–22.

19. George, *Elevating the Game*, 103–31.

20. See Glen Jeansonne, *Leander Perez: Boss of the Delta* (Jackson: University Press of Mississippi, 1977).

21. See Michael L. Kurtz and Morgan D. Peoples, *Earl K. Long: The Saga of Uncle Earl and Louisiana Politics* (Baton Rouge: Louisiana State University Press, 1990); A. J. Liebling, *The Earl of Louisiana* (1961; repr., Baton Rouge: Louisiana State University Press, 2008); and Michael L. Kurtz, "Earl Long's Political Relations with the City of New Orleans, 1948–1960," *Louisiana History* 10 (Summer 1969): 241–54.

22. Alan Wieder, "The New Orleans School Crisis of 1960: Causes and Consequences," *Phylon* 48 (2nd Qtr. 1987): 122–31.

23. Wieder, "New Orleans School Crisis of 1960," 122–31; Juliette Landphair, "Sewerage, Sidewalks, and Schools: The New Orleans Ninth Ward and Public School Desegregation," *Louisiana History* 40 (Winter 1999): 35–62; Diane T. Manning and Perry Rogers, "Desegregation of the New Orleans Parochial Schools," *Journal of Negro Education* 71 (Winter–Spring 2002): 31–42; and *Bush v. Orleans Parish School Board*, 138 F.Supp. 337 (1956).

24. See Maureen Smith, "New Orleans, New Football League, and New Attitudes:

The American Football League All-Star Game Boycott, January 1965," in *Sports and the Racial Divide: African American and Latino Experience in an Era of Change*, ed. Michael E. Lomax (Jackson: University Press of Mississippi, 2008), 3–22; and Gregory L. Richard and Thomas Aiello, "Called Off, On Account of Darkness: The AAU, the AFL, and Civic Development in Jim Crow New Orleans," in *New Orleans Sports*, ed. Thomas Aiello (Fayetteville: University of Arkansas Press, 2019).

25. The full ownership group included Downey, Smither, L. Torrey Gomila, Ronnie Kole, James A. Ware, and Lionel Cunningham. Sixteenth Census of the United States, Population Schedule, New Orleans City, Ward 14, p. 11A; *Times-Picayune* (New Orleans), May 4, 1958, 1, May 12, 1965, 2-8, May 20, 1965, 1-22, May 31, 1965, 1-18, March 28, 1966, 2-3, March 18, 1966, 3-14, December 7, 1966, 1-15, February 1, 1967, 2-8, March 7, 1967, 2-2, November 2, 1967, 1-7; James Gill, *Lords of Misrule: Mardi Gras and the Politics of Race in New Orleans* (Jackson: University Press of Mississippi, 1997), 213; Lake Charles *American-Press*, June 17, 1966, 6; Edward F. Haas, *Mayor Victor H. Schiro: New Orleans in Transition, 1961–1970* (Jackson: University Press of Mississippi, 2014), 85; and Adam Fairclough, *Race & Democracy: The Civil Rights Struggle In Louisiana, 1915–1972* (Athens: University of Georgia Press, 1995), 254, 525.

26. *States-Item* (New Orleans), February 6, 1967, 18, February 17, 1967, 19.

27. Pettit, who was a bank executive in his life after basketball, chose to stay in the financial world. *Atlanta Constitution*, February 5, 1967, 56; and *Times-Picayune* (New Orleans), February 4, 1967, 2-4.

28. *Washington Post*, February 4, 1967, D3.

29. The brash Downey made Pradd the offer after seeing the Dillard star score fifty points against Philander Smith. *Times-Picayune* (New Orleans), February 17, 1967, 2-10, February 18, 1967, 2-9, February 19, 1967, 6-2; and *States-Item* (New Orleans), February 16, 1967, 17.

30. Downey also interviewed Dolph Schayes and Harry Gallatin for the head coaching position. *Washington Post*, May 24, 1967, D4; *Times-Picayune* (New Orleans), February 20, 1967, 4-1; and *States-Item* (New Orleans), February 18, 1967, 10.

31. *Times-Picayune* (New Orleans), March 10, 1967, 2-6; *States-Item* (New Orleans), March 3, 1967, 18; and *Washington Post*, March 5, 1967, C4.

32. Kyle Veazey, *Champions for Change: How the Mississippi State Bulldogs and Their Bold Coach Defied Segregation* (Charleston: History Press, 2012), 79.

33. Ibid., 81–107. See also Dean W. Colvard, *Mixed Emotions: As Racial Barriers Fell, a University President Remembers* (Danville, IL: Interstate Printers and Publishers, 1985).

34. *Times-Picayune* (New Orleans), March 5, 1967, 6-3; *Washington Post*, March 5, 1967, C4; and *Atlanta Constitution*, March 3, 1967, 53.

35. *Washington Post*, July 29, 1967, E5.

36. Davidson, *Breaking the Game Wide Open*, 40–43, 46–47; and *Times-Picayune* (New Orleans), March 6, 1967, 4-1.

37. Downey also made news for drafting pole vault champion Bob Seagren from USC, who had never played college basketball. "He is a great athlete," Downey said, defending the choice, "and we think he can play pro basketball." Downey also defended the trade for Pradd, explaining that the team thought he would be available later in the draft, and therefore did not pick him originally. *Times-Picayune* (New Orleans), April 3, 1967, 4-1, 4-2; *Atlanta Constitution*, April 3, 1967, 39; *New York Times*, April 3, 1967, 43; and *Washington Post*, April 4, 1967, D1.

38. See Thomas Aiello, "You're In the South Now, Brother: The Atlanta Hawks and Race, 1968–1970." *Georgia Historical Quarterly* 98 (Fall 2014): 155–91.

39. *Louisiana Weekly*, January 21, 1967, 2-6, February 11, 1967, 1-6, May 20, 1967, 2-8, September 16, 1967, 3-9, September 23, 1967, 2-7, 2-8, October 14, 1967, 2-8.

40. Charles H. Martin, *Benching Jim Crow: The Rise and Fall of the Color Line in Southern College Sports, 1890–1980* (Urbana: University of Illinois Press, 2010), 219–20; and Michael Martin, "New Orleans Becomes a Big-League City: The NFL-AFL Merger and the Creation of the New Orleans Saints," in *Horsehide, Pigskin, Oval Tracks, and Apple Pie: Essays on Sports and American Culture*, ed. Jim Vlasich (Jefferson, NC: McFarland, 2006), 119–31.

41. *Times-Picayune* (New Orleans), June 23, 1967, 2-12, October 26, 1967, 3-20; and Downey and Hoffer, *Mort! Mort! Mort!*, 84–85.

42. Loyola University *Maroon*, March 17, 1967, 6, May 5, 1967, 11; and *Times-Picayune* (New Orleans), May 3, 1967, 2-7, May 4, 1967, 3-1. The Coliseum Arena would ultimately close in 1960. It was not an option for the Bucs.

43. Father Joseph Malloy to Father Homer R. Jolley, January 26, 1967, Homer R. Jolley Papers, University Archives, Loyola University New Orleans.

44. H. R. Jolley to Members of the Board of Regents, March 23, 1967, and Charles I. Denechaud to Homer R. Jolley, March 27, 1967, Homer R. Jolley Papers.

45. Joseph Malloy to Sean Morton Downey Jr., April 1, 1967, and Lease, September 13, 1967, Homer R. Jolley Papers.

46. *Times-Picayune* (New Orleans), May 23, 1967, 2-8, May 24, 1967, 2-5; and *Atlanta Constitution*, May 23, 1967, 34.

47. *Times-Picayune* (New Orleans), May 27, 1967, 2-6.

48. In 1961, New York City district attorney Frank S. Hogan led a massive investigation into point-shaving associated with the National Invitation Tournament that would ultimately impact as many as fifty players. That scandal eventually made its way down to North Carolina, where athletes from the University of North Carolina and North Carolina State University were investigated. "I was crushed," Moe said of being banned from playing in the NBA. "I didn't know what I was going to do with my life. I always just thought I'd play ball. I had no idea." Ibid., May 28, 1967, 6-8; *Deseret (UT) News*, December 18, 1992, 3-1; and William A. Link, *William Friday: Power, Purpose, and American Higher Education* (Chapel Hill: University of North Carolina Press, 1995), 102–4. Downey's other big target was Boston Celtics forward Bailey Howell, who had played for McCarthy at Mississippi State. He offered Howell a $10,000 raise to jump leagues, but the Celtic would ultimately stay in the NBA. Ibid., May 29, 1967, 3-1; and *Washington Post*, May 24, 1967, D4.

49. *Times-Picayune* (New Orleans), June 2, 1967, 4-1.

50. Ibid., June 5, 1967, 4-3.

51. Sensitive to player motivations, the Royals renegotiated Love's contract and paid him close to what the Bucs were offering. Bob Love and Mel Watkins, *The Bob Love Story: If It's Gonna Be, It's Up To Me* (Chicago: Contemporary Books, 2000), 91–92; *Washington Post*, June 21, 1967, D1, D3, August 22, 1967, D4; and *New York Times*, June 21, 1967, 52.

52. *Times-Picayune* (New Orleans), May 24, 1967, 1-11, June 14, 1967, 4-3, June 16, 1967, 4-1.

53. *Washington Post*, August 5, 1967, D2; and ibid., July 17, 1967, 1-13, August 5, 1967, 2-6.

54. *Times-Picayune* (New Orleans), November 12, 1967, 6-9.

55. Pluto, *Loose Balls*, 75–79. Quote from 77; and Gary Smith, "The Man Who Moved Too Much," *Sports Illustrated*, June 30, 2004, 74–86.

56. Dillard retired Pradd's no. 10 jersey in December of his first professional season, and the *Weekly* covered that, as well. *Louisiana Weekly*, October 7, 1967,

2-8, October 24, 1967, 2-7, December 9, 1967, 2-7, March 2, 1968, 2-9, March 9, 1968, 2-8.

57. Pluto, *Loose Balls*, 75–79. Quote from 77; *Times-Picayune* (New Orleans), June 4, 1967, 6-4, June 5, 1957, 1-11; and Smith, "Man Who Moved Too Much," 74–86.

58. Pluto, *Loose Balls*, 63–64.

59. Ibid., 64.

60. Like Moe, Hawkins had been kept from the NBA as a result of rumors of a betting scandal while he played at the University of Iowa. But he would become the ABA's best player nevertheless. Ibid., 82–83; Chuck O'Donnell, "One Season of Glory," *Basketball Digest*, May 2003, 16; and *Louisiana Weekly*, March 30, 1968, 2-8, April 6, 1968, 2-9, April 13, 1968, 2-9, April 20, 1968, 2-6, April 27, 1968, 2-6, May 4, 1968, 2-9, May 11, 1968, 2-8.

61. Despite the crowd at the final game, the gate receipts had been so small throughout the season that the team moved to Minnesota following year. O'Donnell, "One Season of Glory," 16–17.

62. Pluto, *Loose Balls*, 87, 104–5.

63. Ibid., 90–91, 107. Quote from 90.

64. Ibid., 106–7.

65. Ibid., 75–79. Quote from 77; and Smith, "Man Who Moved Too Much," 74–86.

66. *Atlanta Constitution*, August 7, 1970, 1D, September 1, 1970, 3C; *States-Item* (New Orleans), August 7, 1970, 14, August 8, 1970, 8; *New York Times*, September 1, 1970, 41; *Washington Post*, August 7, 1970, D4, September 1, 1970, 47; and Pluto, *Loose Balls*, 200.

67. *Louisiana Weekly*, May 11, 1968, 2-9, September 21, 1968, 2-9, September 28, 1968, 2-9, October 5, 1968, 2-9, October 19, 1968, 2-10.

68. Ibid., April 5, 1969, 2-9, April 12, 1969, 2-6, April 26, 1969, 2-8, May 10, 1969, 2-8, 2-9, 2-10, September 5, 1970, 2-10, September 12, 1970, 2-7.

69. Memphis originally called itself the Pros. The team had already spent money on the Bucs uniforms and wanted a name that would allow the players' gear to be altered simply and cheaply. Pluto, *Loose Balls*, 239; and "Franchise Snapshot: Memphis Pros . . . Tams . . . Sounds," *Basketball Digest*, November 2001, 18.

70. *States-Item* (New Orleans), September 22, 1970, 13, September 24, 1970, 14, September 26, 1970, 22, September 29, 1970, 19.

71. Zoglin and Tynan, "Pit Bull of Talk-Show Host Morton Downey Jr. Tells Off His Guests," 76; Downey and Hoffer, *Mort! Mort! Mort!*, 137; and Saxon, "Morton Downey Jr.," B9.

CHAPTER 3

1. Caldwell, *Banned from Basketball*, chaps. 4 and 7. (Caldwell's book is self-published and unpaginated. When citing Cadwell's work, this account will note the chapters from which the material is taken.)

2. Kathryn Jay, *More than Just a Game: Sports In American Life Since 1945* (New York: Columbia University Press, 2004), 79–81.

3. Jay, *More than Just a Game*, 79–81, 82. For more on the relationship between sports and television, see Benjamin G. Rader, *In Its Own Image: How Television Has Transformed Sports* (New York: Free Press, 1984).

4. Denberg, Lazenby, and Stinson, *From Sweet Lou to 'Nique*, 15, 31–32. The development of Sunbelt cities has its own growing historiography, particularly in relation to the South. For examples, see Numan V. Bartley, *The New South, 1945–1980* (Baton Rouge: Louisiana State University Press, 1995); James C. Cobb, *The Selling of the South: The Southern Crusade for Industrial Development, 1936–1990* (Baton Rouge: Louisiana State University Press, 1998); David R. Goldfield, *Cotton Fields and Skyscrapers: Southern City and Region, 1607–1980* (Baton Rouge: Louisiana State University Press, 1982); Thomas W. Hanchett, *Sorting Out the New South City: Race, Class, and Urban Development in Charlotte, 1875–1975* (Chapel Hill: University of North Carolina Press, 1998); Jack Temple Kirby, *Rural Worlds Lost: The American South, 1920–1960* (Baton Rouge: Louisiana State University Press, 1987); and Gavin Wright, *Old South, New South: Revolutions in the Southern Economy Since the Civil War* (New York: Basic Books, 1986). For work specifically on Atlanta, some of it cited in this paper's analysis, see Howard L. Preston, *Automobile Age Atlanta: The Making of a Southern Metropolis, 1900–1935* (Athens: University of Georgia Press, 1979); Charles Rutheiser, *Imagineering Atlanta: The Politics of Place in the City of Dreams* (New York: Verso, 1996); Kevin M. Kruse, *White Flight: Atlanta and the Making of Modern Conservatism* (Princeton, NJ: Princeton University Press, 2005); and Ronald H. Bayor, *Race*

and the Shaping of Twentieth-Century Atlanta (Chapel Hill: University of North Carolina Press, 1996).

5. As Kruse notes, "Although the suburbs were just as segregated as the city—and, truthfully, more so—white residents succeeded in convincing the courts, the nation, and even themselves that this phenomenon represented de facto segregation, something that stemmed not from the race-conscious actions of residents but instead from less offensive issues like class stratification and postwar sprawl." Kruse, *White Flight*, 6–10, quote from 8.

6. Benjamin D. Lisle, *Modern Coliseum: Stadiums and American Culture* (Philadelphia: University of Pennsylvania Press, 2017), 4–6. See also David Andrew Harmon, *Beneath the Image of the Civil Rights Movement and Race Relations: Atlanta, Georgia, 1946–1981* (New York: Garland, 1996), 127–65. For other examples of downtown revitalization projects and their relationship to race, see Stephan Thernstrom, *Poverty, Planning, and Politics in the New Boston: The Origins of ABCD* (New York: Basic Books, 1969); Gregory J. Crowley, *The Politics of Place: Contentious Urban Redevelopment in Pittsburgh* (Pittsburgh: University of Pittsburgh Press, 2005); and Neil Smith and Peter Williams, eds., *Gentrification of the City* (Boston: Allen and Unwin, 1986).

7. Robert C. Trumpbour and Kenneth Womack, *The Eighth Wonder of the World: The Life of Houston's Iconic Astrodome* (Lincoln: University of Nebraska Press, 2016), ix–xi, 19–32. Quote from ix. For more on stadia as a function of urban renewal, see Lisle, *Modern Coliseum*, 193–228.

8. Five years later, Cousins would field the expansion Flames in the National Hockey League to fill more dates at the Omni, the arena he would eventually build. This team, too, was a foreign animal to the sports-loving population of Atlanta, and unlike the Hawks, it wouldn't stay. Denberg, Lazenby, and Stinson, *From Sweet Lou to 'Nique*, 15, 31–32.

9. Ibid., 17–18; and "William P. Gates," Naismith Memorial Basketball Hall of Fame website, accessed December 5, 2012, http://www.hoophall.com/hall-of-famers/tag/william-p-gates. See also Bob Kuska, *Hot Potato: How Washington and New York Gave Birth to Black Basketball and Changed America's Game Forever* (Charlottesville: University of Virginia Press, 2004).

10. Denberg, Lazenby, and Stinson, *From Sweet Lou to 'Nique*, 17–18.

11. Aram Goudsouzian, "Bill Russell and the Basketball Revolution," *American Studies* 47 (Fall–Winter 2006): 66; and Denberg, Lazenby, and Stinson, *From Sweet Lou to 'Nique*, 19–23.

12. Barry Gottehrer, "When Wilt and Russell . . . ," *Sport*, March 1960, 38–40; and Goudsouzian, "Bill Russell and the Basketball Revolution," 63, 65, 68. Goudsouzian's article has since been expanded into a book. For a broader treatment of Russell and his relationship to the intersection of race and basketball, see Aram Goudsouzian, *King of the Court: Bill Russell and the Basketball Revolution* (Berkeley: University of California Press, 2010).

13. Russell, *Go Up for Glory*, 166, 168–70; and Devaney, "Pro Basketball's Hidden Fear," 32–33.

14. Russell, *Go Up for Glory*, 166, 168–70, 208–13. Goudsouzian, "Bill Russell and the Basketball Revolution," 73–74; Devaney, "Pro Basketball's Hidden Fear," 32–33, 89–90; and "Hidden Fear That Is Not Our Fear," 104.

15. Russell, *Go Up for Glory*, 120–21.

16. David Halberstam, *The Breaks of the Game* (New York: Knopf, 1981), 146; and Denberg, Lazenby, and Stinson, *From Sweet Lou to 'Nique*, 24.

17. The italics are his. Halberstam, *Breaks of the Game*, 146–47.

18. Russell, *Go Up for Glory*, 155, 163.

19. Denberg, Lazenby, and Stinson, *From Sweet Lou to 'Nique*, 24–25.

20. Halberstam, *Breaks of the Game*, 147–48; and Denberg, Lazenby, and Stinson, *From Sweet Lou to 'Nique*, 27.

21. Pluto, *Loose Balls*, 3–4.

22. That lack of publicity shrouded the next year's sale in secrecy, but it also sped negotiations. It involved a collection of quick decisions. Carl Sanders learned that Kerner was selling the Hawks in early April, and Cousins went to St. Louis to meet with him on April 15. It was a hurried affair, to say the least. "Carl Sanders is so accomplished at keeping secrets that he almost kept his location among the Kentucky Derby crowd just among a few friends," wrote the *Atlanta Journal*'s Furman Bisher, "which isn't easy for a man whose name is constantly creeping into vice-presidential conversation." Halberstam, *Breaks of the Game*, 145; Denberg, Lazenby, and Stinson, *From Sweet Lou to 'Nique*, 28–29; *New York Times*, January 4, 1967, 73, January 15, 1967, 58; *Washington Post*, January 4, 1967, E2, February 1,

1967, D2, January 9, 1967, C1, January 13, 1967, C3; and *Atlanta Journal*, May 6, 1968, 1C.

23. *Atlanta Daily World*, May 10, 1968, 7. The sale was also announced the day after Bill Russell led the Celtics to their ninth title in ten years and—more ominously—the day after the NFL's Atlanta Falcons announced that preseason ticket sales had dropped precipitously because of a poor showing in the team's first season. Denberg, Lazenby, and Stinson, *From Sweet Lou to 'Nique*, 31; *New York Times*, May 4, 1968, 52; *Washington Post*, May 4, 1968, D2; and *Atlanta Journal*, May 3, 1968, 6D, 8D.

24. For more on the riots following the King assassination, see Clay Risen, *A Nation On Fire: America in the Wake of the King Assassination* (Hoboken, NJ: Wiley, 2009).

25. Harry Edwards, *The Revolt of the Black Athlete* (New York: Free Press, 1969), 38–69, 91–114; Amy Bass, *Not the Triumph but the Struggle: The 1968 Olympics and the Making of the Black Athlete* (Minneapolis: University of Minnesota Press, 2002), 81–130; and Tommie Smith, "Why Negroes Should Boycott," *Sport*, March 1968, 40–41, 68.

26. The work on Muhammad Ali is effusive to the point of ubiquity, but perhaps the best biographical treatment—or, at least, the most helpful for this brief account—is David Remnick, *King of the World: Muhammad Ali and the Rise of an American Hero* (New York: Vintage, 1999).

27. Bayor, *Race and the Shaping of Twentieth-Century Atlanta*, 6–7, 12.

28. Bayor, *Race and the Shaping of Twentieth-Century Atlanta*, 6–7, 12, 27, 29; Larry Keating, *Atlanta: Race, Class, and Urban Expansion* (Philadelphia: Temple University Press, 2001), 41–44; and Maurice J. Hobson, "The Dawning of the Black New South: A Geo-Political, Social, and Cultural History of Black Atlanta, Georgia, 1966–1996" (PhD diss., University of Illinois, 2009), 2–3.

29. *Atlanta Journal*, May 6, 1968, 1A. For more on the state of race rights and protests supporting them, see Stephen G. N. Tuck, *Beyond Atlanta: The Struggle for Racial Equality in Georgia, 1940–1980* (Athens: University of Georgia Press, 2001), 192–243.

30. Despite the prospect of overextension, Jackson remained hopeful about the civic prospects of sports. "I mask no fears in writing that the Braves, Chiefs,

Atlanta Falcons, Atlanta Hawks have immeasurably resurrected us in the sense of Rip Van Winkle of Washington Irving renown." *Atlanta Daily World*, May 7, 1968, 1, 4, May 22, 1968, 5.

31. Carl Sanders actually had a large role to play in securing the use of Alexander Memorial. He had appointed many of the school's regents while governor. Ultimately, he was the variable that the Atlanta Falcons lacked, allowing the Hawks to have more favorable relations with the school than did the city's professional football team. Denberg, Lazenby, and Stinson, *From Sweet Lou to 'Nique*, 32; and Richard Hyatt, interview with Thomas Aiello, December 11, 2013.

32. Such was a common pattern with southern universities. Texas Western was the first historically white southwestern university to include black basketball players. In 1966, the school started five black players against lily-white Kentucky and won the NCAA championship. In 1965, TCU became the first Southwest Conference school to integrate its basketball team. Baylor and Arkansas would follow in 1967. In the Southeastern Conference, Vanderbilt desegregated its basketball team in 1966, Auburn in 1967. Alabama would follow in 1969, and Georgia in 1970. "Vice President for Institute Diversity: Timeline," Georgia Institute of Technology website, accessed December 5, 2012, http://www.diversity .gatech.edu/50thanniversary/timeline; and Charles H. Martin, "Jim Crow in the Gymnasium: The Integration of College Basketball in the American South," in *Sport and the Color Line: Black Athletes and Race Relations in Twentieth Century America*, ed. Patrick B. Miller and David K. Wiggins (New York: Routledge, 2003), 241, 243–45.

33. Mark Kriegel, *Pistol: The Life of Pete Maravich* (New York: Free Press, 2007), 180; Denberg, Lazenby, and Stinson, *From Sweet Lou to 'Nique*, 32; Caldwell, *Banned from Basketball*, chap. 7; and *Atlanta Journal*, May 7, 1968, 5D.

34. The Georgia Tech Board of Regents formally approved the agreement with the Hawks on May 8. *Atlanta Journal*, May 4, 1968, 1B, 3B, May 8, 1968, 1D.

35. Ibid., May 5, 1968, 11H, May 6, 1968, 22A, May 8, 1968, 8D.

36. The Omni didn't actually open until October 1972, the start of the NBA season, and therefore the 1972 Democratic National Convention was held in Miami. Ibid., May 6, 1968, 1A; and Robert Coram and Remer Tyson, "The Loser Who Won," *Atlanta Magazine*, November 1970, 43.

37. *Atlanta Journal*, May 5, 1968, 1H, May 16, 1968, n.p., May 17, 1968, n.p.

38. A similar kind of guarded optimism emerged among the region's college coaches. "It really should help all of us to have that kind of basketball in the area," said Auburn's Bill Lynn. "They (the pros) will probably be looking more to Southeastern area college players as prospects, and over-all interest in basketball should be helped a great deal." Ibid., May 4, 1968, 1B, May 5, 1968, 2H, 11H.

39. Or, as J. Richard Munro, publisher of *Sports Illustrated*, would argue, "Players from the NBA Hawks, most of them black, were apprehensive at first about their shift to Atlanta from St. Louis. But the team management, assisted by Bill Bridges, put on a PR (for 'player relations') campaign that assuaged the team's fears." J. Richard Munro, "Letter from the Publisher," *Sports Illustrated*, August 24, 1970, 6.

40. Lou Woodruff was friends with Tom Cousins and an assistant football coach at Georgia Tech. Cousins turned over the Hawks' on-the-ground operations to Woodruff prior to the team's actual move. Woodruff knew Hyatt from Tech and hired him for the public relations job. Hyatt, interview.

41. Caldwell, *Banned from Basketball*, chap. 7.

42. When the Hawks traveled to Seattle in late October, however, Wilkens and the Supersonics drubbed the visitors from the South, 123–112. Wilkens scored 21 points, Hazzard 12. Denberg, Lazenby, and Stinson, *From Sweet Lou to 'Nique*, 33; Caldwell, *Banned from Basketball*, chap. 6; Halberstam, *Breaks of the Game*, 148; *Atlanta Daily World*, October 15, 1968, 5; and *Atlanta Journal*, May 5, 1968, 5H, 9H, May 7, 1968, 4D, August 11, 1968, 4D, August 15, 1968, n.p., September 6, 1968, n.p., September 13, 1968, n.p., September 17, 1968, n.p., September 26, 1968, n.p.

43. The Hawks took Phil Wagner of Georgia Tech in the sixth round, Oscar Smith in the seventh, and Mac Daughtry of Albany State in the ninth. The only non-southerners were Martin Biatti from Manhattan College and Phil Harris from the University of Texas, El Paso. The draft seemed all the more surprising because Blake was considered a master of scouting. "We make up a list of a couple hundred of the nation's best high school seniors each spring," he explained. "Two years later we look for their names to appear in the rosters of the college teams and if they don't, we start searching for them." It was, he noted, an involved process. Halberstam, *Breaks*

of the Game, 147; Denberg, Lazenby, and Stinson, *From Sweet Lou to 'Nique*, 33; and *Atlanta Journal*, May 5, 1968, 5H, May 8, 1968, 1D, May 9, 1968, 1C.

44. And then there was the trial of Lou Hudson. Hudson signed with both the St. Louis Hawks and the Minnesota Muskies of the ABA. He honored the Hawks contract. The Muskies moved to Miami, and the cash-strapped team sued the Hawks over the Hudson double-signing. Though the transaction occurred under the reign of Kerner, the suit fell upon the heads of Cousins and Sanders. The Miami hearing would take place in mid-September as the Hawks were beginning training camp. Hudson requested in US district court that he have a jury trial to determine whether he would play in Atlanta or Miami. His strategy ultimately worked; he played in Atlanta. *Atlanta Journal*, May 7, 1968, 4D, June 9, 1968, 7H, July 15, 1968, n.p., August 15, 1968, 3D, August 28, 1968, n.p., September 4, 1968, n.p., October 15, 1968, n.p.; and *New York Times*, July 28, 1968, 148.

45. Hyatt, interview.

46. That slow start would ultimately bring Guerin off the bench to reprise his role as player-coach. After fifteen games, the team had a losing record. In a game at Cincinnati against the Royals, Guerin suited up and played briefly. Ultimately, he would compete in twenty-seven games during the season, adding another white player to the roster. "Atlanta Hawks at Cincinnati Royals Box Score, November 18, 1968," Basketball Reference website, accessed November 30, 2013, http://www .basketball-reference.com/boxscores/196811160CIN.html; and "1968–69 Atlanta Hawks Schedule and Results," Basketball Reference website, accessed November 30, 2013, http://www.basketball-reference.com/teams/ATL/1969.html. Description of the season comes from the *Atlanta Journal*, which reported on each game. For more information on the Lakers loss, see *Atlanta Journal*, December 7, 1968, 1B. For more on the twelve-game winning streak, see *Atlanta Journal*, January 4, 1969, 1B.

47. The Hawks defeated the San Diego Rockets in the first round of the NBA play-offs in late March and early April 1969 in order to face the Lakers. *Atlanta Journal*, November 7, 1968, n.p., March 25, 1969, 1C, March 26 ,1969, 1C; Denberg, Lazenby, and Stinson, *From Sweet Lou to 'Nique*, 35; and Alfred Wright, "Brave Words from a Hawk and a Warrior," *Sports Illustrated*, March 24, 1969, 26–28, 33–34, 37.

48. For example:

SILAS

Season	Age	Tm	Lg	G	MP	FG	FGA	FG%	TRB	AST	PF	PTS
1964–65	21	STL	NBA	79	1,243	140	375	.373	576	48	161	363
1965–66	22	STL	NBA	46	586	70	173	.405	236	22	72	175
1966–67	23	STL	NBA	77	1,570	207	482	.429	669	74	208	527
1967–68	24	STL	NBA	82	2,652	399	871	.458	958	162	243	1,097
1968–69	25	ATL	NBA	79	1,853	241	575	.419	745	140	166	686
1969–70	26	PHO	NBA	78	2,836	373	804	.464	916	214	266	996

GREGOR

Season	Age	Tm	Lg	G	MP	FG	FGA	FG%	TRB	AST	PF	PTS
1968–69	23	PHO	NBA	80	2,182	400	963	.415	711	96	249	885
1969–70.	24	ATL	NBA	81	1,603	286	661	.433	397	63	159	660

Despite being only two years his senior, Silas had played four more seasons than Gregor. Moreover, Silas was by far a more complete player, outrebounding and outassisting his white counterpart. His 1,097 points in the 1967–68 season dipped in his first Atlanta campaign. But even with his emphasis on rebounding and assisting, Silas maintained a points-per-forty-minutes average almost identical to Gregor's. After Gregor's one disappointing season with Atlanta, the team shipped the forward to Portland. Denberg, Lazenby, and Stinson, *From Sweet Lou to 'Nique*, 35; *Atlanta Journal*, May 9, 1969, 1D; "Paul Silas," Basketball Reference website, accessed 10 November 2012, http://www.basketball-reference.com /players/s/silaspa01.html; and "Gary Gregor," Basketball Reference website, accessed November 10, 2012, http://www.basketball-reference.com/players/g /gregoga01.html. See also Frank DeFord, "Goodbye to the Old Balance of Power," *Sports Illustrated*, October 27, 1969, 30–31.

49. *Atlanta Journal*, October 16, 1968, n.p., April 8, 1969, 3C, May 7, 1969, 1D, June 18, 1969, 4C.

50. "1969–70 Atlanta Hawks Schedule and Results," Basketball Reference website, accessed October 3, 2013, http://www.basketball-reference.com/teams /ATL/1970_games.html; *Atlanta Journal* November 14, 1969, 2D, November 15, 1969, 1B, February 1, 1970, 3C, 7C, February 2, 1970, 1C, 4C, 5C, February 4, 1970,

3D; Denberg, Lazenby, and Stinson, *From Sweet Lou to 'Nique*, 34; Kriegel, *Pistol*,
191; Frank DeFord, "Beware of the Hawks," *Sports Illustrated*, April 13, 1970, 22–27;
and *New York Times*, March 21, 1970, 48. This emphasis of playing to a white
southern audience had a far more overt precursor earlier in the decade. George
Preston Marshall, owner of the Washington Redskins football team, refused
to draft black players in order to curry favor with segregationists in Virginia
and points south. Of course, the Hawks did draft black players, and the federal
government didn't have to pressure them to do so (as it did Marshall), but the
emphasis on whiteness as a source of marketing had been clearly established. See
Thomas G. Smith, *Showdown: JFK and the Integration of the Washington Redskins*
(Boston: Beacon, 2011).

51. *Atlanta Daily World*, October 16, 1968, 2, October 31, 1968, 5.

52. Ibid., April 2, 1969, 3.

53. Ibid., March 28, 1969, 2, April 10, 1969, 8, April 20, 1969, 8, April 2, 1970, 6,
April 5, 1970, 6, April 16, 1970, 9, April 17, 1970, 5, August 3, 1970, 17, 19, August 9,
1970, 10.

54. Denberg, Lazenby, and Stinson, *From Sweet Lou to 'Nique*, 34.

55. Kriegel, *Pistol*, 181.

56. Kent also offered Press Maravich a job in the front office. But he rejected it,
telling his old friend, "I'm not riding on the kid's coattails." Still, Kent was able to
debunk many of Carolina's lavish promises. Ibid., 179–80, 182; and Frank DeFord,
"Merger, Madness and Maravich," *Sports Illustrated*, April 6, 1970, 29–33.

57. After the Hawks drafted Maravich, Jim Gardner, Carolina's owner, went on
the attack. "Tom Cousins will think Quantrill's Raiders were a bunch of amateurs
if Atlanta lucks out and signs Pete Maravich." The Confederate imagery was telling,
but the prediction was wrong. Cousins sold Maravich on the better competition of
the NBA, counting on the athlete's ego to bring him over. Denberg, Lazenby, and
Stinson, *From Sweet Lou to 'Nique*, 34; and Kriegel, *Pistol*, 183–85.

58. Win shares, a sabermetric baseball statistic developed by Bill James in 2002,
has since been applied to professional basketball. It attempts to assign individual
credit for team wins, a figure generally calculated by dividing marginal offense
by marginal points per win. Marginal offense is equivalent to a player's points
produced minus league points per possession multiplied by a player's offensive
possessions.

59. The *Daily World* reported on Maravich's successful senior season at LSU and his honor as the Naismith Player of the Year, which was presented at the Atlanta Tipoff Club. The paper also mentioned his signing with the Hawks, but it again left the team's activities to the mainstream press. *Atlanta Daily World*, March 26, 1970, 6, March 29, 1970, 10; "1970 NBA Draft," Basketball Reference website, accessed November 10, 2012, http://www.basketball-reference.com/draft/NBA_1970.html; Denberg, Lazenby, and Stinson, *From Sweet Lou to 'Nique*, 34; and "Dan Hester," Basketball Reference website, accessed November 10, 2012, http://www.basketball -reference.com/players/h/hesteda01.html.

60. Denberg, Lazenby, and Stinson, *From Sweet Lou to 'Nique*, 34–35; and Caldwell, *Banned from Basketball*, chap. 7.

61. Kriegel, *Pistol*, 191, 197–99.

62. His 3,667 collegiate points in his three varsity seasons is far and away the most points ever scored by a Division I college player. Ibid., 167–80; and *New York Times*, January 6, 1988, B4.

63. Kriegel, *Pistol*, 197–99.

64. Ibid., 193–94, 195–96, 200; and Denberg, Lazenby, and Stinson, *From Sweet Lou to 'Nique*, 35–36. George Preston Marshall's Washington Redskins had used much the same strategy, not playing "Dixie" at the games, but instead changing the words to Washington's fight song from "Fight for Old DC" to "Fight for Old Dixie." Smith, *Showdown*, 141. For more on the Redskins as a predecessor to the Hawks, see note 50.

65. "1970–71 Atlanta Hawks Schedule and Results," Basketball Reference website, accessed October 3, 2013, http://www.basketball-reference.com/teams /ATL/1971_games.html; and Jesse Outlar, "A Year to Forget," *Atlanta Constitution*, September 8, 1971, 1B.

66. Peter Carry, "We Have a Slight Delay in Show Time," *Sports Illustrated*, October 26, 1970, 28–29.

67. Kriegel, *Pistol*, 199–200, 210; and Frank DeFord, "The Hawks: Fouled Up But Flourishing," *Sports Illustrated*, March 8, 1971, 26–28.

68. The New Orleans Jazz, the second Deep South NBA team, would mimic Atlanta in its approach, taking advantage of conflict in Atlanta to acquire Maravich and build its team around a marketable white player. Halberstam, *Breaks of the*

Game, 79; Kriegel, *Pistol*, 208–9; and Denberg, Lazenby, and Stinson, *From Sweet Lou to 'Nique*, 36.

69. *Atlanta Journal*, May 5, 1968, 11H.

70. "Two Pamphlets," Box III-4, folder 46, Carl E. Sanders Papers, Richard B. Russell Library for Political Research and Studies, University of Georgia Libraries, Athens, GA; and Coram and Tyson, "Loser Who Won," 62–63.

71. Randy Sanders, "The Sad Duty of Politics: Jimmy Carter and the Issue of Race in His 1970 Gubernatorial Campaign," *Georgia Historical Quarterly* 76 (Fall 1992): 613–14, 615. For more on the Wallace campaign in the 1968 election, see Dan T. Carter, *The Politics of Rage: George Wallace, the Origins of the New Conservatism, and the Transformation of American Politics* (Baton Rouge: Louisiana State University Press, 1995); Lewis L. Gould, *1968: The Election that Changed America* (New York: Ivan R. Dee, 1993); and Stephan Lesher, *George Wallace: American Populist* (New York: DaCapo, 1994). For more on Maddox, see Bob Short, *Everything Is Pickrick: The Life of Lester Maddox* (Macon: Mercer University Press, 1999); Justin Nystrom, "Segregation's Last Stand: Lester Maddox and the Transformation of Atlanta," *Atlanta History* 45 (Summer 2001): 35–51; and Bruce Galphin, *The Riddle of Lester Maddox* (Atlanta: Camelot, 1968).

72. Sanders, "Sad Duty of Politics," 614–15, 617–20; Kenneth E. Morris, *Jimmy Carter: American Moralist* (Athens: University of Georgia Press, 1996), 178–88; "Platform: Jimmy Carter for Governor, 1970," and "Analysis of Carter Platform," Box III-2, folder 6, Carl E. Sanders Papers; and Jimmy Carter Pre-Presidential Papers, 1962–1976, Accession No. 80-1, Box 38, Sanders, Carl, Jimmy Carter Library, Atlanta, GA.

73. C. B. King was a veteran of the Southern Christian Leadership Conference's Albany Movement and one of the few black lawyers in Georgia practicing outside of Atlanta. Betty Glad, *Jimmy Carter: In Search of the Great White House* (New York: W. W. Norton, 1980) 127, 128, 133, 135; Sanders, "Sad Duty of Politics," 615, 618, 621–22, 624–25, 628; Steven Brill, "Jimmy Carter's Pathetic Lies," *Harper's*, March 1976, 79; "Won't Forget Carter Tactics, Sanders Promises," *Savannah Morning News*, August 28, 1970, 1, Box III-1, folder 23, Carl E. Sanders Papers; "Jimmy Carter Will Be Your Kind of Governor," Jimmy Carter Pre-Presidential Papers, 1962–1976, Accession No. 80-1, Box 23, Campaign Flyers; "Jimmy Carter, September 23, 1970,

Brochure—Gen Election," Jimmy Carter Pre-Presidential Papers, 1962–1976, Accession No. 80-1, Box 23, Campaign Platform 1970; James Clotfelter and William R. Hamilton, "Electing a Governor in the Seventies," in *The American Governor in Behavioral Perspective*, ed. Thad Beyle and J. Oliver Williams (New York: Harper and Row, 1972), 34–35; Leslie Wheeler, *Jimmy Who? An Examination of Presidential Candidate Jimmy Carter: The Man, His Career, His Stands on the Issues* (Middlebury, NY: Barron's, 1976), 53; "Carter's Bitterness Taints His Credibility," *Macon (GA) News*, August 31, 1970, 4A, Box III-1, folder 28, Carl E. Sanders Papers; "Memo to: Jimmy Carter, from: Mike Kelly, re: Title IV—Civil Rights Act of 1964," Jimmy Carter Pre-Presidential Papers, 1962–1976, Accession No. 80-1, Box 25, Civil Rights Act 1964; "Memo to: Jimmy Carter, from: Mike Kelly, re: School Desegregation," Jimmy Carter Pre-Presidential Papers, 1962–1976, Accession No. 80-1, Box 38, School Desegregation; and James F. Cook, *Carl Sanders: Spokesman of the New South* (Macon: Mercer University Press, 1993), 317–39.

74. The Hawks flyer ploy was a revision of an old Eugene Talmadge trick. In one of his gubernatorial campaigns, Talmadge hired a look-alike of his opponent and commissioned him to drive around the state with two black men. *Atlanta Constitution*, June 11, 1970, 17A; Sanders, "Sad Duty of Politics," 627–28; Morris, *Jimmy Carter: American Moralist*, 187; James Wooten, *Das. her: The Roots and the Rising of Jimmy Carter* (New York: Summit Books, 1978), 295; Steven F. Hayward, *The Real Jimmy Carter* (Washington, DC: Regnery, 2004), 49; Reg Murphy and Hal Gulliver, *The Southern Strategy* (New York: Charles Scribner's Sons, 1971), 184–85; and Phil Stanford, "The Most Remarkable Piece of Fiction Jimmy Carter Ever Read," *Columbia Journalism Review* 15 (July/August 1976): 16.

75. Glad, *Jimmy Carter*, 134–35; Victor Lasky, *Jimmy Carter: The Man & the Myth* (New York: Richard Marek, 1979), 77–78; and Bill Shipp, "Stoner Visits Klan, Carter Gives Sermon," *Atlanta Constitution*, July 27, 1970, n.p.

76. Lasky, *Jimmy Carter*, 75–76.

77. According to at least one account, Carter felt guilty about the tactic and called Sanders to apologize. Brill, "Jimmy Carter's Pathetic Lies," 79–80; and Wooten, *Dasher*, 295.

78. "The fiery, sometimes personal attacks launched by Carter against Sanders never alluded to race," wrote the *Constitution*'s Bill Shipp. "But, mysteriously, thousands of leaflets cropped up all over the state in parsonage mailboxes, barber

shops and beauty parlors, linking Sanders socially with Negroes." Lasky, *Jimmy Carter*, 75–76; and Bill Shipp, "White Man's Candidate: Despite Disclaimer, Race Was Big Issue," *Atlanta Constitution*, November 9, 1970, 1A, 12A.

79. In his 1975 autobiography, Carter argued that a vitriolic speech attacking the Atlanta press for making him seem like a rural rube was the reason black voters did not support him. "I was the only candidate who visited all the communities in cities," he argued, "and who spent a large part of my time within the predominantly black stores, restaurants, and street areas." Lasky, *Jimmy Carter*, 76, 78; and Jimmy Carter, *Why Not the Best?* (Nashville: Broadman, 1975), 103.

80. Kriegel, *Pistol*, 219–20; *Atlanta Constitution*, March 30, 1971, 2A; and *Atlanta Journal*, March 30, 1971, 2A, October 16, 1972, 1D.

81. That said, attendance was still poor compared to the more established teams in the league. Atlanta found itself in nineteenth place out of twenty-three teams. Still, attendance was more than 100,000 people higher than it was when the arena opened a decade prior. "1976–77 Atlanta Hawks Roster and Stats," Basketball Reference website, accessed October 2, 2013, http://www.basketball -reference.com/teams/ATL/1977.html; "Atlanta Hawks Franchise Index," Basketball Reference website, accessed October 3, 2013, http://www.basketball -reference.com/teams/ATL/; "1985–86 Atlanta Hawks Roster and Stats," Basketball Reference website, October 3, 2013, http://www.basketball-reference .com/teams/ATL/1986.html; "Dominique Wilkins," Basketball Reference website, accessed October 3, 2013, http://www.basketball-reference.com/players/w /wilkido01.html; and "NBA & ABA All-Star Game Contest Winners," Basketball Reference website, accessed October 3, 2013, http://www.basketball-reference .com/allstar/contest.html.

82. There was a significant racial component to that convention, as white Atlantans expressed fear that Jesse Jackson and his cohort would spread divisiveness and might even provoke riots in the city. Nora Sayre, "Atlanta," *Grand Street* 8 (Spring 1989): 207–9.

83. Benjamin G. Rader, *American Sports: From the Age of Folk Games to the Age of Televised Sports*, 6th ed. (Upper Saddle River, NJ: Prentice Hall, 2009), 240–42; Russell, *Go Up for Glory*; Harry Edwards, *The Revolt of the Black Athlete* (New York: Free Press, 1969); Dave Meggyesy, *Out of Their League* (Lincoln: University of Nebraska Press, 1970); Jim Bouton, *Ball Four: My Life and Hard Times Throwing the*

Knuckleball in the Big Leagues (New York: World, 1970); and Jack Scott, *The Athletic Revolution* (New York: Free Press, 1971).

84. It is significant that Phoenix received an expansion team the year Atlanta bought the Hawks. Soon, other Sunbelt cities like San Diego, Denver, Salt Lake City, San Antonio, Houston, and Dallas would have NBA teams as well. Halberstam, *Breaks of the Game*, 79, 80, 148. For more on the modern outgrowth of the black image in the NBA, see Boyd, "Day the Niggaz Took Over," 123–42.

CHAPTER 4

1. Andrew Romano, "Pancakes and Pickaninnies: The Saga of Sambo's, The 'Racist' Restaurant Chain America Once Loved," *Daily Beast*, June 30, 2014, http ://www.thedailybeast.com/articles/2014/06/30/pancakes-and-pickaninnies -the-saga-of-sambo-s-the-racist-restaurant-chain-america-once-loved.html. See Charles Bernstein, *Sambo's: Only a Fraction of the Action; The Inside Story of a Restaurant Empire's Rise and Fall* (Burbank: National Literary Guild, 1984).

2. Commissioner Walter Kennedy was less committal. "Something concrete may or may not" come from the meeting, he explained. *Times-Picayune* (New Orleans), March 6, 1974, 3-10, March 7, 1974, 3-4; *States-Item* (New Orleans), March 9, 1974, A-8; and *Maroon*, March 21, 1974, 12.

3. *Times-Picayune* (New Orleans), March 7, 1974, 3-5.

4. *Shreveport Times*, March 13, 2015, B5; Frank P. Jozsa Jr., *The National Basketball Association: Business, Organization and Strategy* (Hackensack, NJ: World Scientific, 2011), 32; and *Times-Picayune* (New Orleans), March 1, 1974, 1, 3. In response to not getting the hoped-for merger, and in hopes of eventually getting it, the ABA announced the following month that it would hold a five-round draft wherein its teams would draft existing NBA players. "I have no comment except to say that I assume the ABA would not attempt to have an NBA player breach his existing contract," replied a frustrated Walter Kennedy. Ibid., April 13, 1974, 2-6.

5. *Times-Picayune* (New Orleans), March 9, 1974, 2-8. New Orleans was the only expansion team added to the association, and it was the first franchise to enter the NBA without a counterpart. The NBA placed New Orleans in the Central Division with the Atlanta Hawks, Washington Bullets, Houston Rockets, and Cleveland Cavaliers. *Times-Picayune* (New Orleans), March 30, 1974, 2-7.

6. *States-Item* (New Orleans), March 9, 1974, A-9, March 11, 1974, C-4.

7. Tulane's Charles Moir was more guarded in his comments. "It will affect us in one of two ways," he said. "It will either help or hurt. I hope it serves as a stimulus for our program." *Times-Picayune* (New Orleans), March 8, 1974, 2-4. For more on the Superdome's construction as compared with other stadia in the second half of the twentieth century, see Lisle, *Modern Coliseum*, 238–43.

8. *Louisiana Weekly*, March 16, 1974, 2-6, March 23, 1974, 2-9, 2-11, April 6, 1974, 2-11, April 20, 1974, 1-9.

9. *Times-Picayune* (New Orleans), March 9, 1974, 2-6. See "Filing No. R0000, Street No. 01500, Poydras St., Louisiana Superdome, 1970/11/16, Permit No. 91600, Architect: Curtis and Davis, Edward B. Silverstein and Associates," Building Plans In the City Archives, City Archives, New Orleans Public Library.

10. *Maroon*, March 21, 1974, 12; and *Times-Picayune* (New Orleans), March 11 1974, 3.

11. Jep Cadou, "New Orleans' Dome Sweet Dome," *Saturday Evening Post*, April 1975, 62.

12. *Times-Picayune* (New Orleans), February 15, 1975, 1, 10, February 16, 1975, 1, 22, February 19, 1975, 1, 5.

13. See "Superdome, Louisiana (I)," "Superdome, Louisiana (11)," vertical file, Louisiana Division, New Orleans Public Library; and Ibid., 25 March 1975, 10, March 27, 1975, 8, June 29, 1975, 1, 14.

14. *Times-Picayune* (New Orleans), *DIXIE Magazine*, 3 August 1975, 11.

15. *Times-Picayune* (New Orleans), April 14, 1974, 2. See "Municipal Auditorium," Richard Remy Dixon (1911–1991) Papers, ca. 1958–1977, MS 326, Manuscripts Collection, Louisiana Division, New Orleans Public Library. The extant records for Municipal only cover the period from 1927 to 1973, prior to the Jazz's brief tenure in the building. Nevertheless, these documents demonstrate the auditorium's place as the logical landing spot for the team as it waited for the Superdome to be completed. See Records of the Municipal Auditorium, City Archives, New Orleans Public Library.

16. *Maroon*, March 14, 1974, 15. The auditorium needed no remodeling for basketball, as it had undergone a relatively extensive renovation a few years prior in 1968. Improvements to Municipal included the addition of new concession stands and additional seating space, making it ready for its new professional

residents. "Filing No. R0269, Street No. 01201, St. Peter St., Municipal Auditorium, Additions, Repairs and Alterations, 1966/09/21, Permit No. 67030, Architect: Mathes, Bergman, Favrot and Associates," "Filing No. R0181, Street No. 01201, St. Peter St., Municipal Auditorium, Repairs, Alterations, and Additions— Phase II, 1968/02/09, Permit No. 74820, Architect: Mathes, Bergman, Favrot and Associates," "Filing No. R0188, Street No. 01201, St. Peter St., Municipal Auditorium, Concessions, 1968/02/19, Permit No. 74952, Architect: Mathes, Bergman, Favrot and Associates," Building Plans in the City Archives.

17. Hot Rod Hundley and Tom McEachin, *Hot Rod Hundley: You Gotta Love It, Baby* (Champaign, IL: Sports Publishing, 1998), 155.

18. *Maroon*, March 21, 1974, 12.

19. *Times-Picayune* (New Orleans), May 19, 1974, 6-2.

20. Ibid., March 17, 1974, 6-2.

21. Kriegel, *Pistol*, 230–31.

22. *Maroon*, October 3, 1974, 8; and *Times-Picayune* (New Orleans), April 25, 1974, 5-1, 5-2.

23. *Times-Picayune* (New Orleans), April 26, 1974, 4-1, April 27, 1974, 2-6, April 28, 1974, 2.

24. Kriegel, *Pistol*, 230.

25. *Maroon*, October 3, 1974, 8; and *Times-Picayune* (New Orleans), May 4, 1974, 4-1, 4-3.

26. *Times-Picayune* (New Orleans), May 5, 1974, 6-1, May 10, 1974, 2-14.

27. *Louisiana Weekly*, May 4, 1974, 2-6, May 11, 1974, 2-8.

28. *States-Item* (New Orleans), May 7, 1974, A-13, May 8, 1974, D-1.

29. Hundley and McEachin, *Hot Rod Hundley*, 156.

30. *Times-Picayune* (New Orleans), May 20, 1974, 2-6.

31. Hundley and McEachin, *Hot Rod Hundley*, 157; *States-Item* (New Orleans), March 19, 1974, C-1; and *Times-Picayune* (New Orleans), May 9, 1974, 6-1, May 28, 1974, 2-8.

32. *Los Angeles Times*, March 16, 2008, D-4. Bertka stayed almost exclusively in Santa Barbara, CA, far from the team and New Orleans, not helping the team's success. "More than Pete Maravich, the player, more than Scottie Robertson, the head-coach designate, more than Fred Rosenfeld, the president of the franchise," wrote Peter Finney, "the man who probably means success or failure for this city's

NBA team is one of those non-stop dynamos, who lives out of a suitcase, whose office hours blur, who is a good customer of the airlines and the phone company. His name is Bill Bertka." New Orleans *States-Item*, May 9, 1974, A-14; and Kriegel, *Pistol*, 239.

33. Hundley and McEachin, *Hot Rod Hundley*, 153–55; *States-Item* (New Orleans), April 19, 1974, C-1; and *Shreveport Times*, March 13, 2015, B5.

34. The location is now the Jung Hotel. *Times-Picayune* (New Orleans), May 19, 1974, 6-5; and Hundley and McEachin, *Hot Rod Hundley*, 153.

35. *States-Item* (New Orleans), May 10, 1974, C-1; and *Times-Picayune* (New Orleans), May 21, 1974, 3-1, 3-7.

36. Ibid.

37. *Times-Picayune* (New Orleans), May 29, 1974, 3-8; and *States-Item* (New Orleans), March 20, 1974, B-12. Because of the Maravich trade, the team's second season was its first with a first-round draft pick. The Jazz selected seven-foot Stanford center Rich Kelley. Kelley was white, and while his race might have been a factor in the selection, he was a solid player slated to be drafted in roughly that position. In the second round, the team drafted Jim McElroy, a black guard who played collegiately at Central Michigan but was from Arkansas. Hundley and McEachin, *Hot Rod Hundley*, 158.

38. *Times-Picayune* (New Orleans), June 8, 1974, 4-1. One alternate suggestion was the Pigeons, a letter writer arguing that the birds were "the first to inhabit the Superdome." Carrier pigeons were originally used to get pictures of football games from Tulane Stadium to newspaper offices to meet deadlines. The correspondent also stated, "Pigeons have a nuisance value that will always provoke uneasy thoughts with the opposition." *States-Item* (New Orleans), May 14, 1974, A-11.

39. Hundley and McEachin, *Hot Rod Hundley*, 157; and *Times-Picayune* (New Orleans), June 17, 1974, 3-12, June 18, 1974, 4-1, June 20, 1974, 6-1, 6-3, June 21, 1974, 4-1.

40. *Times-Picayune* (New Orleans), June 21, 1974, 4-1.

41. "Super Dome problems," Box 7, Tape 8, Subject 4, 11/16/75, Joseph Culotta Jr. Collection, Audio Tapes, 1975, Manuscripts Collection, Louisiana Division, New Orleans Public Library; and Ibid., August 6, 1974, 5, August 25, 1974, 6-4, August 27, 1974, 3-1.

42. After Baylor, the Jazz added Celtics legend Sam Jones to the coaching staff. *Times-Picayune* (New Orleans), September 12, 1974, 5-1, September 14, 1974, 2-6, September 18, 1974, 4-8.

43. Hundley and McEachin, *Hot Rod Hundley*, 155.

44. *Times-Picayune* (New Orleans), August 18, 1974, 6-3, October 9, 1974, 3-1, October 10, 1974, 2-8; and *Maroon*, October 3, 1974, 8.

45. *Times-Picayune* (New Orleans), October 25, 1974, 2-1. The team began its life with an eleven-game losing streak and lost its first fifty road games, never coming close to a winning season while in New Orleans. "New Orleans Jazz," *Basketball Digest*, December 2002, 1.

46. Kriegel, *Pistol*, 240.

47. Ibid., 235; Jozsa, *National Basketball Association*, 32; and *Times-Picayune* (New Orleans), April 26, 1975, 2-1.

48. *Times-Picayune* (New Orleans), August 29, 1975, 1-7.

49. Ibid., February 14, 1976, 2-5.

50. Hundley and McEachin, *Hot Rod Hundley*, 156. See "Jabbar slam dunk," Rowles Stereograph Collection, Louisiana State Museum, accession # 1979.120.282, available at Louisiana Digital Library, accessed May 2, 2017, http://cdm16313 .contentdm.oclc.org/cdm/singleitem/collection/RSP/id/265/rec/9.

51. "New Orleans Jazz (Basketball Team)," vertical file, Louisiana Division, New Orleans Public Library; and Kriegel, *Pistol*, 241.

52. New Orleans *Times-Picayune*, September 29, 1975, 6.

53. Ibid., September 29, 1975, 6, October 8, 1975, 1, 14.

54. Ibid., October 14, 1975, 1, 14, November 4, 1975, 6.

55. Ibid., November 11, 1975, 1, 6.

56. Ibid., November 13, 1975, 1, 10, November 16 , 1975, 1, 10, 28.

57. Tulane's protest had its genesis in higher ticket and concession prices than its previous on-campus venue had charged. Fans could not bring their own alcohol, and they couldn't go onto the field. In addition, the Green Wave got very little practice time in the Superdome. Ibid., November 17, 1975, 2, November 18, 1975, 1, 14.

58. Ibid., November 18, 1975, 14, November 20, 1975, 1, 19, November 22, 1975, 1, 4.

59. Ibid., December 28, 1975, 8, January 13, 1976, 3.

60. Ibid., January 25, 1976, 8-6, 8-14, 8-15.

61. Ibid., January 28, 1976, 4, February 5, 1976, 1, 12.

62. Ibid., December 30, 1976, 1, 4, December 31, 1976, 1, 8, January 8, 1977, 3.

63. Ibid., August 24, 1976, 3, May 18, 1977, 1, May 20, 1977, 8, June 2, 1977, 14, June 3, 1977, 4, October 11, 1977, 1, 17, October 12, 1977, 1, October 15, 1977, 1, 17, October 21, 1977, 4, October 25, 1977, 1, 8, November 4, 1977, 1, 20.

64. Ibid., November 11, 1977, 8, November 16, 1977, 8.

65. Ibid., June 14, 1977, 3-1, June 16, 1977, 3-1; and Lee H. Schlesinger, et al. v. Corporate Realty Inc. et al., 2 F.3d 135 (5th Cir. 1993).

66. The fans would be able to keep their hard-drinking coach, as he would later become the coach of the city's first professional women's basketball team, the Pride, in 1980. Peter Finney's response to the absence of the Jazz and the knowledge that the city would get its first professional women's team was, "The kings are dead. Long live the queens." New Orleans *States-Item*, June 4, 1979, C1; Kriegel, *Pistol*, 247. For more on Van Breda Kolff and the Pride, see Stacy Tanner, "'In Spite of Ourselves' They Were the Pride of New Orleans: The Role of Race, Gender, and the Media in the Demise of the Crescent City's Women's Professional Basketball Franchise, 1979–1981," in *New Orleans Sports*, ed. Thomas Aiello (Fayetteville: University of Arkansas Press, 2019).

67. *Times-Picayune* (New Orleans), December 7, 1977, 3-1; and "1976–77 New Orleans Jazz Roster and Stats," Basketball-Reference website, accessed April 29, 2017, http://www.basketball-reference.com/teams/NOJ/1977.html; "1977–78 New Orleans Jazz Roster and Stats," Basketball-Reference website, accessed April 29, 2017, http://www.basketball-reference.com/teams/NOJ/1978.html; and "1978–79 New Orleans Jazz Roster and Stats," Basketball-Reference website, accessed April 29, 2017, http://www.basketball-reference.com/teams/NOJ/1979.html.

68. Hundley and McEachin, *Hot Rod Hundley*, 157; and Kriegel, *Pistol*, 254–56.

69. Robinson would go on to average 15.8 rebounds per game in the 1977–78 season. This mark was the best ever for the Jazz and the high mark for that season, making him the only player in team history to lead the NBA in rebounding. "New Orleans Jazz," *Basketball Digest*, December 2002, 1; Hundley and McEachin, *Hot Rod Hundley*, 157; and Kriegel, *Pistol*, 254–56, 262–63.

70. *Louisiana Weekly*, October 12, 1974, 2-6, October 19, 1974, 2-8, October 26, 1974, 2-8, November 2, 1974, 2-6, August 30, 1975, 2-6.

71. Ibid., October 12, 1974, 2-6, October 19, 1974, 2-8, October 26, 1974, 2-8, November 2, 1974, 2-6, August 30, 1975, 2-6, January 24, 1976, 2-7, February 7, 1976, 2-6, May 28, 1977, 2-11, June 25, 1977, 2-10, July 2, 1977, 2-8, April 3, 1979, 2-7.

72. Ibid., April 21, 1979, 2-6. The *Weekly* never reported on the team's move to Utah. It just began referring to the Utah Jazz in brief mentions of the team later in 1979. June 30, 1979, 2-7.

73. "Superdome Schedule, 1975–1985," Box 2, Senator Sidney J. Barthelemy Collection, MS 323, Manuscripts Collection, Louisiana Division, New Orleans Public Library; and *Times-Picayune* (New Orleans), April 12, 1979, 12.

74. *Washington Post*, February 20, 1970, D5, April 24, 1970, D8; *Christian Science Monitor*, February 28, 1970, 6; *New York Times*, April 8, 1970, 74, April 17, 1970, 63; and Jozsa, *National Basketball Association*, 35.

75. The team's basic argument was that since Hyatt was not part of the original lease when the team signed with the Superdome, the original lease was now invalid. *Times-Picayune* (New Orleans), April 12, 1979, 1.

76. Ibid., April 11, 1979, 2-1, April 12, 1979, 7-1.

77. *States-Item* (New Orleans), April 12, 1979, D7; and Ibid., April 13, 1979, 2-1, April 14, 1979, 1-11.

78. *Times-Picayune* (New Orleans), April 15, 1979, 1, 5, April 19, 1979, 4-1, April 20, 1979, 2-1; and *States-Item* (New Orleans), April 17, 1979, C1, C2.

79. *Times-Picayune* (New Orleans), April 24, 1979, 4-1; and *States-Item* (New Orleans), May 1, 1979, C1.

80. *Times-Picayune* (New Orleans), April 24, 1979, 4-1, May 15, 1979, 4-1; and *States-Item* (New Orleans), May 1, 1979, C1.

81. "Save Our Jazz Committee (basketball team)," May 4, 1979, Tape 12, Side 2, Sound Recordings: 1978–1985, Box G27, Sub-series I—Press Conferences, Intergovernmental Relations Administration, Public Information Office Records, Mayor Ernest N. Morial Records, City Archives, New Orleans Public Library; and *Times-Picayune* (New Orleans), May 5, 1979, 4-1.

82. *States-Item* (New Orleans), May 5, 1979, B1; and *Times-Picayune* (New Orleans), May 6, 1979, 40, 6-1, May 9, 1979, 15.

83. *Times-Picayune* (New Orleans), May 31, 1979, 1, 4-1, June 1, 1979, 2-1, June 2, 1979, 1, May 4, 1979, 16; and *States-Item* (New Orleans), May 11, 1979, C1, May 16, 1979, E1, May 31, 1979, C1, C3, June 1, 1979, C1, C7.

84. *Times-Picayune* (New Orleans), April 13, 1979, 1, 17, June 2, 1979, 1, June 4, 1979, 3-1.

85. Ibid., July 6, 1979, 1, 11, July 7, 1979, 2-1.

86. *Wall Street Journal*, May 30, 1979, 18; and *Times Picayune* (New Orleans), April 14, 1979, 1, April 23, 1979, 1, June 4, 1979, 3-1.

87. Jozsa, *National Basketball Association*, 33; and *Times-Picayune* (New Orleans), June 9, 1979, 1, 9, June 10, 1979, 6-1.

88. *Times-Picayune* (New Orleans), May 20, 1979, 6-2, June 13, 1979, 4-1. Rumors about new teams in New Orleans began immediately, the one with the most traction being speculation that Eddie DeBartolo, who would later own the San Francisco 49ers, would buy the Cleveland Cavaliers and move them to New Orleans. DeBartolo called the rumors "very premature," but he didn't deny them. Ibid., June 15, 1979, 3-2.

89. Ibid., July 13, 1979, 1, July 23, 1979, 6, July 26, 1979, 4-1, July 28, 1979, 3-1, July 31, 1979, 2-2.

90. Ibid., August 2, 1979, 1, 10, August 3, 1979, 2-2, August 4, 1979, 2-2, August 30, 1979, 1.

91. Romano, "Pancakes and Pickaninnies"; *New York Times*, March 11, 1981, D4, November 28, 1981, 30; and "A New Name," *Time*, August 17, 1981, 67.

CONCLUSION

1. Joshua D. Bernstein, "Dominique Wilkins (b. 1960)," *New Georgia Encyclopedia*, accessed May 4, 2017, http://www.georgiaencyclopedia.org/articles /sports-outdoor-recreation/dominique-wilkins-b-1960.

2. Bernstein, "Dominique Wilkins (b. 1960)"; and "Dominique Wilkins," Basketball-Reference website, accessed May 4, 2017, http://www.basketball -reference.com/players/w/wilkido01.html.

3. Alton Hornsby Jr., *Black Power in Dixie: A Political History of African Americans in Atlanta* (Gainesville: University Press of Florida, 2009), 183–209, quotes from 186, 208–9; Harmon, *Beneath the Image of the Civil Rights Movement and Race Relations*, 277–79; Peter Ross Range, "Making It in Atlanta: Capital of Black-is-Beautiful," *New York Times Magazine*, April 7, 1974, 21–29, 68–78; and Phyl Garland, "Atlanta, Black Mecca of the South," *Ebony*, August 1970, 152–57.

4. Hornsby, *Black Power in Dixie*, 183–209, quotes from 186, 208–9.

5. "Atlanta Braves Team History," Baseball-Reference website, accessed August 21, 2017, https://www.baseball-reference.com/teams/ATL/index.shtml; and "Atlanta Falcons Franchise Encyclopedia," Football-Reference website, accessed August 21, 2017, https://www.pro-football-reference.com/teams/atl/.

6. *Houston Chronicle*, December 4, 1986, 1.

7. Fort Lauderdale *Sun Sentinel*, September 24, 1986, 2C.

8. Paige Williams, "Atlanta According to Dominique Wilkins," *Atlanta*, November 2007, 348.

9. Fort Lauderdale *Sun Sentinel*, April 2, 1989, 3C, April 5, 1989, 2C; *Chicago Tribune*, April 2, 1989, 6; and *Orlando Sentinel*, April 5, 1989, C4.

10. *Atlanta Constitution*, May 9, 1989, D3; and "Hawks Trade Dominique Wilkins to Clippers for Danny Manning," *Jet*, March 21, 1994, 40.

11. *Atlanta Daily World*, December 15, 1988, 8. For examples of the near-ubiquitous coverage in the city's black newspaper, see *Atlanta Daily World*, July 20, 1986, 8, September 25, 1986, 8, January 25, 1987, 8, August 21, 1988, 8, February 9, 1989, 7, August 24, 1989, 1.

12. Bayor, *Race and the Shaping of Twentieth-Century Atlanta*, 259.

13. Kruse, *White Flight*, 234.

14. For a brief summary of the Hawks later racial scandals, see Marc J. Spears, "GM Wes Wilcox Disciplined by Hawks for Racially Charged Remark," ESPN website, accessed August 21, 2017, http://www.espn.com/nba/story/_/id/18446972/atlanta-hawks-disciplined-general-manager-wes-wilcox-racially-charged-remark; and Scott Gleeson, "Atlanta Hawks Face Racial Discrimination Lawsuit," USA Today, July 6, 2017, https://www.usatoday.com/story/sports/nba/hawks/2017/07/06/atlanta-hawks-face-racial-discrimination-lawsuit/456100001/.

15. Miami also received a franchise and began play in 1988, but its population demographics in the late 1980s were far different from the rest of the South's. Still, the success of the NBA in markets like Atlanta unquestionably paved the way for the Heat as well. "1988–89 Atlanta Hawks Roster and Stats," Basketball-Reference website, accessed May 4, 2017, http://www.basketball-reference.com/teams/ATL/1989.html; New Orleans *Times-Picayune*, December 7, 2012, 4-1; and

"Orlando Magic," NBA website, accessed May 4, 2017, http://stats.nba.com /team/#!/1610612753/seasons/.

16. *Charlotte (NC) Observer*, November 1, 2008, 4-1; *Los Angeles Times*, July 4, 2011, 3-1; *Chicago Tribune*, January 25, 2001, 2-2; and *Toronto Sun*, October 20, 1999, 3-1.

17. *USA Today*, October 30, 2002, 3C. Seeking a more Louisiana-appropriate name, the Hornets would later change their name to the New Orleans Pelicans.

18. "Hawks retire 'Pistol' Pete Maravich's No. 44," NBA website, March 3, 2017, http://www.nba.com/article/2017/03/03/atlanta-hawks-retire-pistol-pete -maravichs-no-44; "New Orleans Hornets at Atlanta Hawks Box Score, November 16, 2002," Basketball-Reference website, accessed May 4, 2017, http://www .basketball-reference.com/boxscores/200211160ATL.html; and "Atlanta Hawks at New Orleans Hornets Box Score, November 27, 2002," Basketball-Reference website, accessed May 4, 2017, http://www.basketball-reference.com/boxscores /200211270NOH.html.

BIBLIOGRAPHY

NEWSPAPERS

Alexandria (LA) *Town Talk*
Atlanta Constitution
Atlanta Daily World
Atlanta Journal
Baltimore Afro-American
Charlotte Observer
Chicago Defender
Chicago Tribune
Christian Science Monitor
Deseret (UT) *News*
Fort Lauderdale Sun Sentinel
Houston Chronicle
Lake Charles (LA) *American-Press*
Los Angeles Sentinel
Los Angeles Times
Louisiana Weekly (New Orleans, LA)
Loyola University *Maroon* (New Orleans, LA)
Macon (GA) *News*
Nashville Tennessean
New Orleans *States-Item*
New Orleans *Times-Picayune*

New York Herald Tribune
New York Times
Orlando Sentinel
Pittsburgh Courier
Savannah Morning News
Shreveport Times
St. Louis *Post-Dispatch*
Toledo Blade
Toronto Sun
USA Today
Wall Street Journal
Washington Post

ARCHIVAL SOURCES

Barthelemy, Senator Sidney J. Collection. MS 323. Manuscripts Collection, Louisiana Division, New Orleans Public Library.
Building Plans in the City Archives. City Archives, New Orleans Public Library.
Carter, Jimmy. Pre-Presidential Papers, 1962–1976. Accession No. 80-1. Jimmy Carter Library, Atlanta, GA.
Culotta, Joseph, Jr. Collection. Audio Tapes, 1975. Manuscripts Collection, Louisiana Division, New Orleans Public Library.
Dixon, Richard Remy, (1911–1991). Papers, ca. 1958–1977. MS 326. Manuscripts Collection, Louisiana Division, New Orleans Public Library.
Harold Weisberg Archive. Hood College, Frederick, MD.
Jolley, Homer R. Papers. University Archives, Loyola University New Orleans.
Morial, Mayor Ernest N. Records. City Archives, New Orleans Public Library.
"New Orleans Jazz (Basketball Team)," vertical file, Louisiana Division, New Orleans Public Library.
Records of the Municipal Auditorium. City Archives, New Orleans Public Library.
Rowles Stereograph Collection. Louisiana State Museum.
Sanders, Carl E. Papers. Richard B. Russell Library for Political Research and Studies, University of Georgia Libraries, Athens, GA.

"Superdome, Louisiana (I)," vertical file. Louisiana Division, New Orleans Public Library.

"Superdome, Louisiana (II)," vertical file. Louisiana Division, New Orleans Public Library.

OTHER PRIMARY SOURCES

Bouton, Jim. *Ball Four: My Life and Hard Times Throwing the Knuckleball in the Big Leagues*. New York: World, 1970.

Bush v. Orleans Parish School Board. 138 F.Supp. 337 (1956).

Cadou, Jep. "New Orleans' Dome Sweet Dome." *Saturday Evening Post*. April 1975. 62.

Caldwell, Joe. *Banned from Basketball: The Long Strange Trip of "Pogo" Joe Caldwell*. Tempe: self-published 2003.

Carry, Peter. "We Have a Slight Delay in Show Time." *Sports Illustrated*. October 26, 1970. 28–29.

Carter, Jimmy. *Why Not the Best?* Nashville: Broadman, 1975.

Coram, Robert, and Remer Tyson. "The Loser Who Won." *Atlanta Magazine*. November 1970. 43.

DeFord, Frank. "Beware of the Hawks." *Sports Illustrated*. April 13, 1970. 22–27.

———. "Goodbye to the Old Balance of Power." *Sports Illustrated*. October 27, 1969. 30–31.

———. "The Hawks: Fouled Up But Flourishing." *Sports Illustrated*. March 8, 1971. 26–28.

———. "Merger, Madness and Maravich." *Sports Illustrated*. April 6, 1970. 29–33.

Devaney, John. "Pro Basketball's Hidden Fear." *Sport*. February 1966. 32–33, 89–92.

Downey, Morton, Jr., and William Hoffer. *Mort! Mort! Mort! No Place to Hide*. New York: Delacorte, 1988.

Edwards, Harry. *The Revolt of the Black Athlete*. New York: Free Press, 1969.

Federal Writers' Project of the Works Progress Administration. *New Orleans City Guide, 1938*. 1938. Reprint. New Orleans: Garret County Press, 2011.

Garland, Phyl. "Atlanta, Black Mecca of the South." *Ebony*. August 1970. 152–57.

Gottehrer, Barry. "When Wilt and Russell . . ." *Sport*. March 1960. 38–40.

"Hawks Trade Dominique Wilkins to Clippers for Danny Manning." *Jet*. March 21, 1994. 40.

"Hidden Fear that Is Not Our Fear, The." *Sport*. May 1966. 104.

Hyatt, Richard. Interview with Thomas Aiello. December 11, 2013.

Lasky, Victor. *Jimmy Carter: The Man & the Myth*. New York: Richard Marek, 1979.

Lee H. Schlesinger et al. v. Corporate Realty Inc. et al. 2 F.3d 135 (5th Cir. 1993).

Munro, J. Richard. "Letter from the Publisher." *Sports Illustrated*. August 24, 1970. 6.

"New Name, A." *Time*. August 17, 1981. 67.

Range, Peter Ross. "Making It in Atlanta: Capital of Black-is-Beautiful." *New York Times Magazine*. April 7, 1974. 21–29, 68–78.

"Raymond Johnson." *Editor and Publisher* 81 (1948): 40.

Russell, Bill. *Go Up for Glory*. New York: Coward-McCann, 1966.

———. "Success Is A Journey." *Sports Illustrated*. June 8, 1970. 80–93.

Scott, Jack. *The Athletic Revolution*. New York: Free Press, 1971.

Sixteenth Census of the United States.

Smith, Tommie. "Why Negroes Should Boycott." *Sport*. March 1968. 40–41, 68.

Stanford, Phil. "The Most Remarkable Piece of Fiction Jimmy Carter Ever Read." *Columbia Journalism Review* 15 (July/August 1976): 16.

Turner, William W. "The Garrison Commission." *Ramparts Magazine*. January 1968. 68–69.

United States v. Clayton Kimble and Jules Ron Kimbel. 719 F.2d 1253 (1983).

Wheeler, Leslie. *Jimmy Who? An Examination of Presidential Candidate Jimmy Carter: The Man, His Career, His Stands on the Issues*. Middlebury, NY: Barron's, 1976.

Williams, Paige. "Atlanta According to Dominique Wilkins." *Atlanta*. November 2007. 348.

Wright, Alfred. "Brave Words from a Hawk and a Warrior." *Sports Illustrated*. March 24, 1969. 26–28, 33–34, 37.

Zoglin, Richard, and William Tynan. "The Pit Bull of Talk-Show Host Morton Downey Jr. Tells Off His Guests—And His Audience." *Time*. January 4, 1988. 76.

SECONDARY SOURCES

Adelson, Bruce. *Brushing Back Jim Crow: The Integration of Minor League Baseball in the American South*. Charlottesville: University of Virginia Press, 2007.

Aiello, Thomas. "The Robinson Interregnum: The Black Press Responds to the Signing of Jackie Robinson, October 23, 1945–March 1, 1946." *Readex Report* 12 (March 2017). www.readex.com.

———. "You're In the South Now, Brother: The Atlanta Hawks and Race, 1968–1970." *Georgia Historical Quarterly* 98 (Fall 2014): 155–91.

Axthelm, Pete. *The City Game: Basketball from the Garden to the Playgrounds*. 1970. Reprint. Lincoln: University of Nebraska Press, 1999.

Bartley, Numan V. *The New South, 1945–1980*. Baton Rouge: Louisiana State University Press, 1995.

Baseball Reference. www.baseball-reference.com.

Basketball Reference. www.basketball-reference.com.

Bass, Amy. *Not the Triumph but the Struggle: The 1968 Olympics and the Making of the Black Athlete*. Minneapolis: University of Minnesota Press, 2002.

Bayne, Bijan C. *Elgin Baylor: The Man Who Changed Basketball*. Lanham, MD: Rowman and Littlefield, 2015.

Bayor, Ronald H. *Race and the Shaping of Twentieth-Century Atlanta*. Chapel Hill: University of North Carolina Press, 1996.

Bernstein, Charles. *Sambo's: Only a Fraction of the Action; The Inside Story of a Restaurant Empire's Rise and Fall*. Burbank: National Literary Guild, 1984.

Bernstein, Joshua D. "Dominique Wilkins (b. 1960)." *New Georgia Encyclopedia*. Accessed May 4, 2017. www.georgiaencyclopedia.org.

Black, Jack, Robert Bradley, and Al Kirk. "History of the Southern Basketball League." Association for Professional Basketball Research website. Accessed June 20, 2016. www.apbr.org

Boyd, Todd. "The Day the Niggaz Took Over: Basketball, Commodity Culture, and Black Masculinity." In *Out of Bounds: Sports, Media, and the Politics of Identity*, edited by Aaron Baker and Todd Boyd, 134–37. Bloomington: Indiana University Press, 1997.

Brill, Steven. "Jimmy Carter's Pathetic Lies." *Harper's*. March 1976. 79.

Carter, Dan T. *The Politics of Rage: George Wallace, the Origins of the New Conservatism, and the Transformation of American Politics*. Baton Rouge: Louisiana State University Press, 1995.

"Chairman of the Board of Governors/Board of Governors." Association for Professional Basketball Research website. Accessed April 1, 2017. www.apbr.org.

Chalk, Oceania. *Pioneers of Black Sport: The Early Days of the Black Professional Athlete in Baseball, Basketball, Boxing, and Football*. New York: Dodd, Mead, 1975.

Clotfelter, James, and William R. "Electing a Governor in the Seventies." In *The American Governor in Behavioral Perspective*, edited by Thad Beyle and J. Oliver Williams, 34–35. New York: Harper and Row, 1972.

Cobb, James C. *The Selling of the South: The Southern Crusade for Industrial Development, 1936–1990*. Baton Rouge: Louisiana State University Press, 1998.

Colvard, Dean W. *Mixed Emotions: As Racial Barriers Fell, a University President Remembers*. Danville, IL: Interstate Printers and Publishers, 1985.

Cook, James F. *Carl Sanders: Spokesman of the New South*. Macon, GA: Mercer University Press, 1993.

Crowley, Gregory J. *The Politics of Place: Contentious Urban Redevelopment in Pittsburgh*. Pittsburgh: University of Pittsburgh Press, 2005.

Davidson, Gary. *Breaking the Game Wide Open*. New York: Atheneum, 1974.

Demas, Lane. *Integrating the Gridiron: Black Civil Rights and American College Football*. New Brunswick: Rutgers University Press, 2011.

Denberg, Jeffrey, Roland Lazenby, and Tom Stinson. *From Sweet Lou to 'Nique*. Atlanta: Longstreet, 1992.

Fairclough, Adam. *Race & Democracy: The Civil Rights Struggle in Louisiana, 1915–1972*. Athens: University of Georgia Press, 1995.

Feinstein, John. *The Punch: One Night, Two Lives, and the Fight that Changed Basketball Forever*. New York: Back Bay Books, 2003.

Figone, Albert J. *Cheating the Spread: Gamblers, Point Shavers, and Game Fixers in College Football and Basketball*. Urbana: University of Illinois Press, 2012.

Football Reference. www.pro-football-reference.com.

"Franchise Snapshot: Memphis Pros . . . Tams . . . Sounds." *Basketball Digest*. November 2001. 18.

Galphin, Bruce. *The Riddle of Lester Maddox*. Atlanta: Camelot, 1968.

George, Nelson. *Elevating the Game: Black Men and Basketball*. New York: HarperCollins, 1992.

Gill, James. *Lords of Misrule: Mardi Gras and the Politics of Race in New Orleans*. Jackson: University Press of Mississippi, 1997.

Glad, Betty. *Jimmy Carter: In Search of the Great White House*. New York: W. W. Norton, 1980.

Goldfield, David R. *Cotton Fields and Skyscrapers: Southern City and Region, 1607–1980*. Baton Rouge: Louisiana State University Press, 1982.

Goudsouzian, Aram. "Bill Russell and the Basketball Revolution." *American Studies* 47 (Fall–Winter 2006): 61–85.

———. *King of the Court: Bill Russell and the Basketball Revolution*. Berkeley: University of California Press, 2010.

Gould, Lewis L. *1968: The Election that Changed America*. New York: Ivan R. Dee, 1993.

Grasso, John. *Historical Dictionary of Basketball*. Lanham, MD: Scarecrow, 2011.

Haas, Edward F. *Mayor Victor H. Schiro: New Orleans in Transition, 1961–1970*. Jackson: University Press of Mississippi, 2014.

Halberstam, David. *The Breaks of the Game*. New York: Knopf, 1981.

Hanchett, Thomas W. *Sorting Out the New South City: Race, Class, and Urban Development in Charlotte, 1875–1975*. Chapel Hill: University of North Carolina Press, 1998.

Harmon, David Andrew. *Beneath the Image of the Civil Rights Movement and Race Relations: Atlanta, Georgia, 1946–1981*. New York: Garland, 1996.

Hayward, Steven F. *The Real Jimmy Carter*. Washington, DC: Regnery, 2004.

Hoberman, John. *Darwin's Athletes: How Sport Has Damaged Black America and Preserved the Myth of Race*. New York: Mariner Books, 1997.

Hobson, Maurice J. "The Dawning of the Black New South: A Geo-Political, Social, and Cultural History of Black Atlanta, Georgia, 1966–1996." PhD diss., University of Illinois, 2009.

Hornsby, Alton, Jr. *Black Power in Dixie: A Political History of African Americans in Atlanta*. Gainesville: University Press of Florida, 2009.

Hundley, Hot Rod, and Tom McEachin. *Hot Rod Hundley: You Gotta Love It, Baby*. Champaign, IL: Sports Publishing, 1998.

Jay, Kathryn. *More than Just a Game: Sports in American Life Since 1945.* New York: Columbia University Press, 2004.

Jeansonne, Glen. *Leander Perez: Boss of the Delta.* Jackson, MS: University Press of Mississippi, 1977.

Jozsa, Frank P., Jr. *The National Basketball Association: Business, Organization and Strategy.* Hackensack, NJ: World Scientific, 2011.

Keating, Larry. *Atlanta: Race, Class, and Urban Expansion.* Philadelphia: Temple University Press, 2001.

Kemper, Kurt Edward. *College Football and American Culture in the Cold War Era.* Urbana: University of Illinois Press, 2009.

Kirby, Jack Temple. *Rural Worlds Lost: The American South, 1920–1960.* Baton Rouge: Louisiana State University Press, 1987.

Kriegel, Mark. *Pistol: The Life of Pete Maravich.* New York: Free Press, 2007.

Kruse, Kevin M. *White Flight: Atlanta and the Making of Modern Conservatism.* Princeton, NJ: Princeton University Press, 2005.

Kurtz, Michael L. "Earl Long's Political Relations with the City of New Orleans, 1948–1960." *Louisiana History* 10 (Summer 1969): 241–54.

Kurtz, Michael L., and Morgan D. Peoples. *Earl K. Long: The Saga of Uncle Earl and Louisiana Politics.* Baton Rouge: Louisiana State University Press, 1990.

Kuska, Bob. *Hot Potato: How Washington and New York Gave Birth to Black Basketball and Changed America's Game Forever.* Charlottesville: University of Virginia Press, 2004.

LaBlanc, Michael L., ed. *Professional Sports Team Histories: Basketball.* Detroit: Gale Research, 1994.

Landphair, Juliette. "Sewerage, Sidewalks, and Schools: The New Orleans Ninth Ward and Public School Desegregation." *Louisiana History* 40 (Winter 1999): 35–62.

Lane, Jeffrey. *Under the Boards: The Cultural Revolution in Basketball.* Lincoln: University of Nebraska Press, 2007.

Leifer, Eric M. *Making the Majors: The Transformation of Team Sports in America.* Cambridge, MA: Harvard University Press, 1995.

Lesher, Stephan. *George Wallace: American Populist.* New York: DaCapo, 1994.

Liebling, A. J. *The Earl of Louisiana.* 1961. Reprint. Baton Rouge: Louisiana State University Press, 2008.

Link, William A. *William Friday: Power, Purpose, and American Higher Education*. Chapel Hill: University of North Carolina Press, 1995.

Lisle, Benjamin D. *Modern Coliseum: Stadiums and American Culture*. Philadelphia: University of Pennsylvania Press, 2017.

Love, Bob, and Mel Watkins. *The Bob Love Story: If It's Gonna Be, It's Up To Me*. Chicago: Contemporary Books, 2000.

Manning, Diane T., and Perry Rogers. "Desegregation of the New Orleans Parochial Schools." *Journal of Negro Education* 71 (Winter–Spring 2002): 31–42.

Marcus, Jeff. *A Biographical Dictionary of Professional Basketball Coaches*. Lanham, MD: Scarecrow, 2003.

Martin, Charles H. *Benching Jim Crow: The Rise and Fall of the Color Line in Southern College Sports, 1890–1980*. Urbana: University of Illinois Press, 2010.

———. "Jim Crow in the Gymnasium: The Integration of College Basketball in the American South." In *Sport and the Color Line: Black Athletes and Race Relations in Twentieth Century America*, edited by Patrick B. Miller and David K. Wiggins, 241–45. New York: Routledge, 2003.

Martin, Michael. "New Orleans Becomes a Big-League City: The NFL-AFL Merger and the Creation of the New Orleans Saints." In *Horsehide, Pigskin, Oval Tracks, and Apple Pie: Essays on Sports and American Culture*, edited by Jim Vlasich, 119–31. Jefferson, NC: McFarland, 2006.

Meggyesy, Dave. *Out of Their League*. Lincoln: University of Nebraska Press, 1970.

Meyer, Roger. "Professional Basketball League of America, 1947–48." Association for Professional Basketball Research website. Accessed June 20, 2016. www.apbr.org.

Morris, Kenneth E. *Jimmy Carter: American Moralist*. Athens: University of Georgia Press, 1996.

Murphy, Reg, and Hal Gulliver. *The Southern Strategy*. New York: Charles Scribner's Sons, 1971.

National Basketball Association website. www.nba.com.

Nelson, Murray R. *Abe Saperstein and the American Basketball League, 1960–1963*. Jefferson, NC: McFarland, 2013.

———. *The National Basketball League: A History, 1935–1949*. Jefferson, NC: McFarland, 2009.

"New Orleans Jazz." *Basketball Digest*. December 2002. 1.

Novak, Michael. *The Joy of Sports: End Zones, Bases, Baskets, Balls, and the Consecration of the American Spirit*. New York: Basic Books, 1976.

Nystrom, Justin. "Segregation's Last Stand: Lester Maddox and the Transformation of Atlanta." *Atlanta History* 45 (Summer 2001): 35–51.

O'Donnell, Chuck. "One Season of Glory." *Basketball Digest*. May 2003. 16.

Pluto, Terry. *Loose Balls: The Short, Wild Life of the American Basketball Association*. New York: Simon and Schuster, 1990.

Posner, Gerald. *Killing the Dream: James Earl Ray and the Assassination of Martin Luther King, Jr.* New York: Random House, 1998.

Preston, Howard L. *Automobile Age Atlanta: The Making of a Southern Metropolis, 1900–1935*. Athens: University of Georgia Press, 1979.

Rader, Benjamin G. *American Sports: From the Age of Folk Games to the Age of Televised Sports*. 6th ed. Upper Saddle River, NJ: Prentice Hall, 2009.

——— . *In Its Own Image: How Television Has Transformed Sports*. New York: Free Press, 1984.

Rampersad, Arnold. *Jackie Robinson: A Biography*. New York: Random House, 1997.

Remnick, David. *King of the World: Muhammad Ali and the Rise of an American Hero*. New York: Vintage, 1999.

Rhoden, William C. *Forty Million Dollar Slaves: The Rise, Fall, and Redemption of the Black Athlete*. New York: Broadway, 2007.

Richard, Gregory L. and Thomas Aiello. "Called Off, On Account of Darkness: The AAU, the AFL, and Civic Development in Jim Crow New Orleans." In *New Orleans Sports*, ed. Thomas Aiello. Fayetteville: University of Arkansas Press, 2019.

Riess, Steven A. *City Games: The Evolution of American Urban Society and the Rise of Sports*. Urbana: University of Illinois Press, 1991.

Risen, Clay. *A Nation On Fire: America in the Wake of the King Assassination*. Hoboken, NJ: Wiley, 2009.

Robertson, Oscar. *The Big O: My Life, My Times, My Game*. New York: Rodale, 2003.

Romano, Andrew. "Pancakes and Pickaninnies: The Saga of Sambo's, The 'Racist' Restaurant Chain America Once Loved." *Daily Beast*. June 30, 2014. www.thedailybeast.com.

Rutheiser, Charles. *Imagineering Atlanta: The Politics of Place in the City of Dreams*. New York: Verso, 1996.

Ryan, Bob. *The Pro Game: The World of Professional Basketball*. New York: McGraw-Hill, 1975.

Sammons, Jeffrey T. "'Race' and Sport: A Critical, Historical Examination." *Journal of Sport History* 21 (Fall 1994): 203–78.

Sanders, Randy. "The Sad Duty of Politics: Jimmy Carter and the Issue of Race in His 1970 Gubernatorial Campaign." *Georgia Historical Quarterly* 76 (Fall 1992): 612–38.

Sayre, Nora. "Atlanta." *Grand Street* 8 (Spring 1989): 207–9.

Schleppi, John. *Chicago's Showcase of Basketball: The World Tournament of Professional Basketball and the College All-Star Game*. Haworth, NJ: St. Johann, 2008.

Short, Bob. *Everything Is Pickrick: The Life of Lester Maddox*. Macon, GA: Mercer University Press, 1999.

Shropshire, Kenneth L. In *Black and White: Race and Sports in America*. New York: New York University Press, 1998.

Silver, James W. *Mississippi: The Closed Society*. 1964. Reprint. Jackson: University Press of Mississippi, 2012.

Smith, Gary. "The Man Who Moved Too Much." *Sports Illustrated*. June 30, 2004. 74–86.

Smith, John Matthew. *The Sons of Westwood: John Wooden, UCLA, and the Dynasty that Changed College Basketball*. Urbana: University of Illinois Press, 2013.

Smith, Maureen. "New Orleans, New Football League, and New Attitudes: The American Football League All-Star Game Boycott, January 1965." In *Sports and the Racial Divide: African American and Latino Experience in an Era of Change*, ed. Michael E. Lomax, 3–22. Jackson: University Press of Mississippi, 2008.

Smith, Neil, and Peter Williams, eds. *Gentrification of the City*. Boston: Allen and Unwin, 1986.

Smith, Thomas G. *Showdown: JFK and the Integration of the Washington Redskins*. Boston: Beacon, 2011.

Surdam, David George. *The Rise of the National Basketball Association*. Urbana: University of Illinois Press, 2012.

Tanner, Stacy. "'In Spite of Ourselves' They Were the Pride of New Orleans: The Role of Race, Gender, and the Media in the Demise of the Crescent City's Women's Professional Basketball Franchise, 1979–1981." In *New Orleans Sports*, ed. Thomas Aiello. Fayetteville: University of Arkansas Press, 2019.

Thernstrom, Stephan. *Poverty, Planning, and Politics in the New Boston: The Origins of ABCD*. New York: Basic Books, 1969.

Thomas, Damion. *Globetrotting: African American Athletes and Cold War Politics*. Urbana: University of Illinois Press, 2012.

Traughber, Bill. *Nashville Sports History: Stories from the Stands*. Charleston: History Press, 2010.

Trumpbour, Robert C., and Kenneth Womack. *The Eighth Wonder of the World: The Life of Houston's Iconic Astrodome*. Lincoln: University of Nebraska Press, 2016.

Tuck, Stephen G. N. *Beyond Atlanta: The Struggle for Racial Equality in Georgia, 1940–1980*. Athens: University of Georgia Press, 2001.

Veazey, Kyle. *Champions for Change: How the Mississippi State Bulldogs and Their Bold Coach Defied Segregation*. Charleston: History Press, 2012.

"Vice President for Institute Diversity: Timeline." Georgia Institute of Technology website. Accessed December 5, 2012. www.diversity.gatech.edu.

Walker, Chet. "On the Road in the South, 1960." In *The Unlevel Playing Field: A Documentary History of the African American Experience in Sport*, edited by David K. Wiggins and Patrick B. Miller, 277–82. Urbana: University of Illinois Press, 2005.

Whiteside, James. *Colorado: A Sports History*. Niwot: University Press of Colorado, 1999.

Widmer, Mary Lou. *New Orleans in the Thirties*. Gretna, LA: Pelican, 1989.

Wieder, Alan. "The New Orleans School Crisis of 1960: Causes and Consequences." *Phylon* 48 (2nd Qtr. 1987): 122–31.

"William P. Gates." Naismith Memorial Basketball Hall of Fame website. Accessed 5 December 2012. www.hoophall.com.

Wooten, James. *Dasher: The Roots and the Rising of Jimmy Carter*. New York: Summit Books, 1978.

Wright, Gavin. *Old South, New South: Revolutions in the Southern Economy Since the Civil War*. New York: Basic Books, 1986.

"Year Round Hockey?" *SportsLetter*. August 5, 1993. 3.

Zirin, Dave. *What's My Name, Fool? Sports and Resistance in the United States*. Chicago: Haymarket Books, 2005.

INDEX

A. Philip Randolph Institute, 105

Aaron, Hank, 59, 75, 76

Abdul-Jabbar, Kareem (Lew Alcindor), ix, 76, 77, 98

Abernathy, Ralph, 67

Abernathy, Ray, 82, 83

Ackerman, James, 45

Agnew, Spiro, 85

Alabama Christian Movement for Human Rights, 18

Albany Movement, 145n

Albany State University, 140

Alexander Memorial Coliseum (Atlanta), 59, 68, 69, 80, 139n

Alger, Horatio, 20

Ali, Muhammad, 66–67, 108, 138n

All-American Girls Professional Baseball League, 124

All-American Red Heads, 16

Allen, Ivan, 60, 62

Allen, Robert, 45

Amateur Athletic Union, 10, 11, 43

American Basketball Association, 72, 74, 94–95, 96, 100, 126n, 134n, 141n
   and blackness, 31, 39, 107
   competition with NBA, ix, 30–31, 38, 65–66
   founded, 38–39
   in the South, 30–31, 77–78

   in New Orleans, ix, 6, 33, 37–38, 43–46, 49–56, 88, 93, 94, 107
   merger with NBA, 1, 89, 99, 109, 148n

American Basketball League, 1, 24

American Broadcasting Company, 28, 78, 80

American Business Club, 22

American Cancer Society, 101

American Football League, 28, 30, 38, 50
   1965 All-Star Game, 4, 41–42

American Heart Association, 101

Anaheim Amigos, 52, 109

Anderzunas, Wally, 74

Archdiocese of New Orleans, 41

Archibald, Tiny, 77

Arizona State University, 59, 73

Arkansas AM&N, 45

Assassin, the, 76

Associated Negro Press, 18

Associated Press, 14

Association for Professional Basketball Research, 127n

Athas, Alex, 15

Athletic Revolution, The, 85

Atlanta Athletic Club, 68

Atlanta Basketball Club, 11

Atlanta Braves, 4, 8, 59, 60, 76, 117, 118–19, 138n

Atlanta Chiefs, 76, 138n